Communication: Apprehension, Avoidance, and Effectiveness

Second Edition

Virginia P. Richmond

James C. McCroskey

West Virginia University

Gorsuch Scarisbrick, Publishers
Scottsdale, Arizona

10 9 8 7 6 5 4 3 2

ISBN 0-89787-331-9

Gorsuch Scarisbrick, Publishers
8233 Via Paseo del Norte, Suite F-400
Scottsdale, AZ 85258

Printed in the United States of America

PREFACE

Human communication has been a focus of concern of scholars for almost 5000 years. The study of human communication has held a central position in the education of the young in most societies throughout recorded history. The purpose of this book is to summarize some of the more recent approaches to understanding the human communication process.

This book will not tell you "everything you always wanted to know about communication but were afraid to ask." Rather, it will provide you with a general introduction to communication and explain why you may have been afraid to ask.

The first chapter is devoted to outlining basic information central to understanding what communication is and how people misunderstand its nature. Chapter 3 focuses on the most widespread communication problem in our society-shyness, what it is and why it occurs. The fourth chapter centers on the primary cause of shyness, communication apprehension.

Chapter 5 summarizes some of the major effects of communication apprehension and avoidance in people's everyday lives while Chapter 6 centers on the effects of communication apprehension and avoidance on communication effectiveness. The final chapter, Chapter 7, explains the various methods that have been developed to help people overcome communication apprehension.

A brief book such as this cannot include all of the information that you might like to obtain in any area. Consequently, we have included numerous references where you can pursue more in-depth knowledge. If you are particularly interested in communication apprehension and avoidance, we suggest you read *Avoiding Communication: Shyness, Reticence, and Communication Apprehension* (1984) which was edited by Daly and McCroskey. This book includes chapters by many of the leading researchers in the area and provides more complete summaries of the relevant information than we can provide here. You should also read the McCroskey and Richmond chapter in *Willingness to Communicate in Personality and Interpersonal Communication* (1987) which was edited by McCroskey and Daly.

We would like to acknowledge a young woman (who must remain nameless) who threatened to commit suicide if she were to be required to give another speech in a speech class and a young man (who also must remain nameless) who regurgitated his lunch when he was required to do so. You made believers out of us. Some people really are deathly afraid to communicate, no matter what our former public speaking teachers told us.

Contents

1

An Overview of Human Communication

In this age of computer literacy and increased attention to communication between people and computers, it might seem as if human-to-human communication has become much less important than it used to be. However, this is not the case. Regardless of the new emphasis on communication with computers, most of our daily interaction is with other people on a live, interpersonal level. Supervisors still communicate with their subordinates on a one-to-one basis. Teachers still communicate with students on a one-to-one basis. And lovers still communicate with each other on a one-to-one basis. Thus, even though computers are playing and will continue to play a significant role in our lives, they will not replace basic human interaction. They will be used in many organizations as the primary mode of transferring information because they are more efficient and faster than the human mind. However, live communication between humans will still be the fuel that makes our world go around.

DEFINITION OF HUMAN COMMUNICATION

Human communication is the process by which a person (or persons) stimulates meaning in the mind of another person (or persons) through use of verbal and/or nonverbal messages. This definition encompasses three types of communication—accidental, expressive, and rhetorical.

Accidental Communication

Accidental communication occurs when a person does not realize he or she has stimulated meaning in the mind of another. This happens more frequently than many people realize. How often have you stimulated meaning in the mind of another person without really trying to do so? For example, you may attend a lecture and about halfway through the lecture yawn several times; the speaker notices this and says something to the effect of, "I must be communicating something boring, the lady in the back row has yawned four times in the last five minutes." Then everyone laughs while you sit there embarrassed.

Most scholars in nonverbal communication suggest that through our nonverbal behaviors we are often accidentally communicating meanings to others when we don't even realize we're communicating. People communicate their needs, interests, desires, likes, dislikes, weaknesses, and so on without having the slightest desire to do so, and often in spite of a definite desire *not* to do so. The way we walk, talk, dress, and present ourselves stimulates meaning in another's mind about who we are and what we are like. This is not only true in the United States, it is universal. For example, in Arab culture it is customary to stand very close and breathe into the other person's face when communicating. Americans find this offensive and often offend their Arab counterparts by backing away during an interaction. The American perceives the Arab as rude and aggressive and the Arab perceives the American as cold and distant. Hence, intercultural business transactions often are conducted by skilled intermediaries so the parties involved do not communicate something they do not mean to communicate.

Most of us realize that, regardless of the emphasis on communication with computers, most of our basic daily interaction is with other people on a live, interpersonal level.   James L. Shaffer

Expressive Communication

Expressive communication occurs from the emotional, or motivational, state of an individual. The messages produced are representative of the individual's feelings at a given time. For example, when typing a paper, if you find you have made a major error that causes you to have to retype several pages of text, you might shout an exclamation such as "darn" that would communicate to another person that you are displeased with your typing skills. If another person is not present, expressive communication cannot occur. No one is present, so no meaning is produced by the message. This type of communication can be intentional or unintentional. Sometimes we purposely stimulate meaning in the mind of another by saying something that expresses our emotional or motivational state, but often we are not even aware we are stimulating meaning in the mind of another.

Rhetorical Communication

McCroskey (1986) defines rhetorical communication as "the process of a source stimulating a source-selected meaning in the mind of a receiver by means of verbal and nonverbal messages" (p. 4). The source is an individual or a group from whom the message emanates. Source-selected meaning is what the source has previously decided he/she wants to create in the mind of the receiver. In order for the source to be successful, the receiver must receive and interpret the message the way the source intends it.

Rhetorical communication is goal directed. The source seeks to produce in the mind of the receiver a *specific* meaning. In this type of communication the source might attempt several ways of getting her/his meaning into the receiver's mind. A source will continue transmitting messages until the receiver reacts the way the source thinks he/she should or the source will simply give up.

Our understanding of the communication process would not be complete without viewing the components necessary for effective communication. The next section of this chapter is devoted to listing and defining the various components in the human communication process.

COMPONENTS OF THE HUMAN COMMUNICATION PROCESS

The process of human communication has seven essential components: source, message, channel, receiver, encoding, decoding, and feedback. A number of models of communication have been developed to illustrate the relationships among these components. One of the first models, developed by Shannon and Weaver (1949), makes no reference to meaning; instead it represents *message-centered communication* (see Figure 1). This model incorporates a source, such as a person, who puts a message into a transmitter, such as a computer, with the message then being transmitted through a channel, such as a telephone wire, to a receiver. Shannon and Weaver also include noise in their model; we will discuss noise later in this chapter.

Berlo (1960) developed the SMCR model of human communication (see Figure 2), which also includes the source, message, channel, and receiver(s). In addition, this model allows for all three types of *meaning-centered communication:* accidental, expressive, and rhetorical. Berlo's model implies that noise is present; however, it is not pictorially represented.

This model considers five elements that might impact communication between sources and receivers: the participants' communication skills, attitudes, and knowledge; the social system of which they are a part; and their cultural environment. This model suggests that the channel is comprised of five primary sensory systems: seeing, hearing, touching, smelling, and tasting.

Both of these models were very good initial attempts at outlining and describing the components in the human communication process. However, both fall short of the goal. The Shannon-Weaver model overlooks the interaction that may take place between source and receiver and fails to focus on meaning stimulated by interactions. The Berlo Model fails to delineate communication as a process, overlooking the idea that receivers, and not just sources, are active participants in the process. In other words, a source does not simply transmit a message with the receiver passively

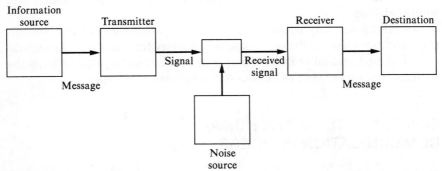

FIGURE 1. The Shannon-Weaver Model of Communication. [*Source:* C.E. Shannon and W. Weaver, *The Mathematical Theory of Communication* (Urbana, IL: University of Illinois Press, copyright ©1949), p. 98. Reprinted by permission of the University of Illinois Press.]

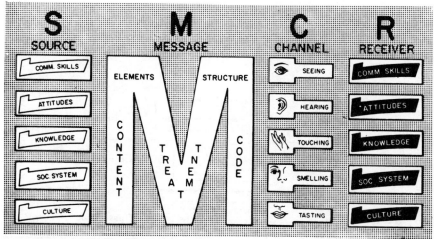

FIGURE 2. Berlo's SMCR Model of Communication. [*Source:* D.K. Berlo, *The Process of Communication* (New York: Holt, Rinehart & Winston, copyright © 1960), p. 72. Reprinted by permission of CBS College Publishing.]

receiving it. Often receivers and sources are equally active as participants in the human communication process. Finally, both models have left out other components that are important to the communication process, such as feedback, which we will discuss in a moment.

The most useful model for our purposes is the model proposed by McCroskey, Larson, and Knapp (1971). Figure 3 shows the basic interpersonal communication model, which incorporates the process notion of communication, taking into account the receiver can be an active participant in the communication process. This model of interpersonal communication recognizes the dual role each communication participant plays, acting as both a source and a receiver. This model also allows for feedback: We see that the channel from person A to person B is the feedback channel for person B and the channel from person B to person A is the feedback channel for person A. Similarly, person A's message is person B's feedback and person B's message is person A's feedback. In this model *feedback* refers to the messages transmitted by the source, formerly called the receiver, to a receiver, formerly called the source. Today, this type of model—that incorporates all of these essential elements of the communication process— is accepted as being most representative of interpersonal communication.

Let us now review the seven essential components illustrated in this model.

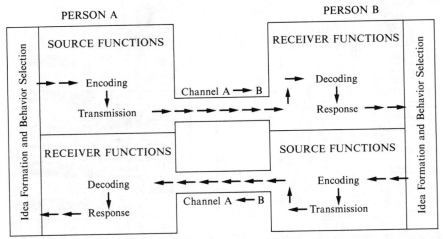

FIGURE 3. Interpersonal Communication Model. [*Source:* From James C. Mc-Croskey, *An Introduction to Rhetorical Communication*, 5th Ed. (Englewood Cliffs, NJ: Prentice-Hall, 1986), p. 12.]

Source

The source is the person (or persons) who originates the message. The source usually performs three functions: determining the meaning to be communicated, encoding the meaning into a message that the receiver can understand, and sending the message. Usually the source is the person sending the message as well as the originator of the message, but this may not always be the case. For example, news reporters are message senders but are not necessarily the originators of the messages they transmit.

The source's functions sound simple, but this is not the case. If a source employs a language code to which the receiver cannot relate, the message might be misunderstood. This is a common problem. For example, the teacher (source) who uses terminology that the student (receiver) does not understand or identify with may not understand why the student fails an exam that employs the same language. This is one reason why representatives of an ethnic group may suggest that a standardized intelligence test does not accurately tap or evaluate the intelligence of all who take the test. The sources of those tests are using the language to which they are accustomed, not necessarily the language used by the groups being tested. As you can see, the functions of the source are critical to effective communication.

Message

The message is any verbal or nonverbal stimulus that may evoke meaning in the mind of the person receiving it. As an example of a nonverbal message, many of us try to communicate a certain image by the clothing we wear. The dress of the military and police communicates authority and may have the effect of commanding respect. The student who comes to class with purple and green hair, heavy makeup, and studded leather bracelets and arm bands is communicating a different type of a message.

A message may be unintentional or intentional. Perhaps the student mentioned above is drawn naturally to such a style of dress or perhaps the student really wants to communicate that he or she is part of a "punk" group.

Messages may be interpreted unconsciously by their receivers. For example, if the door to a supervisor's office is always closed between 9 a.m. and 10 a.m., employees unconsciously learn to refrain from interrupting him/her during that time. Messages may also be very direct. For example, one of the authors of this text doesn't hesitate to tell his faculty that it is budget time and not to disturb him or the secretary who is helping him process the budget.

The message one sends will usually have components of both verbal and nonverbal communication; these two aspects of communication are inextricably linked. Finally, regardless of whether a message has an intended meaning, it may or may not be interpreted as was intended.

Channel

The channel is the means by which the message is conveyed from the source to the receiver. Channels may be sound waves, light waves, the sense of touch or smell, and so on. Many times a message is sent through a combination of channels. For example, when you tell someone you love them while hugging them, you have sent the same message through two different channels. In some situations people serve as channels. For example, a message may be passed from a supervisor to a middle-level manager and then to the employees. If you remember the distorted messages that resulted from the childhood game of "grapevine," when a message was whispered from person to person, then you can identify the biggest problem in a message passing through a "chain" of human channels. People tend to emphasize what is relevant to them, perhaps leaving out other relevant information.

It is important to remember that the channel(s) employed to transmit a message determines the outcome of the interaction.

Receiver

The receiver is the person (or persons) who receives the message. The receiver may be an individual or a group. A message usually has an intended receiver, although there is no guarantee that the intended receiver will be reached; for example, if a television commercial for beer is run during Saturday morning cartoons, it may reach a mass audience but it will certainly not reach the intended audience. (Advertisers spend untold time and energy avoiding such costly mistakes, of course.) There is also no way to ensure that the receiver will interpret the message as was intended (see the discussion of encoding below).

The receiver's interpretation of the source's message determines the type of response the receiver returns. Thus, the receiver too plays a significant role in the human communication process.

Encoding

Encoding is the process of translating an already conceived idea into a message appropriate for transmission to a receiver. The encoding process consists of three parts: creation of the message, adaptation of the message to the intended receiver, and transmission of the message. Effective encoding is dependent upon the source knowing what meaning a certain message will create in the receiver's mind. Sources attempt to use words, colors, sounds, and so on, for their messages that will create the intended meaning in the receiver's mind. Encoding is a receiver-oriented process, whether the receiver is one person or many.

Decoding

Decoding is the process in which the receiver translates or interprets the message(s) he/she receives, and there are four steps to this process. The first step is the receiver *receiving* the message, whether by hearing, seeing, or otherwise sensing it (remember that receipt of a message is usually through a combination of channels). The second step is the receiver determining what he/she thinks the source intended to communicate. This is commonly known as the *interpretation* stage. The third step is the receiver *evaluating* the message in terms of its meaning and relationship to the receiver. The last step is the *formulation of a response* to the source's message by the receiver.

Feedback

This component of the communication process is the receiver's response to the message as it has been seen or heard, interpreted, and evaluated. Feedback may be an overt, observable response, or it may be a covert, nonobservable internal response, or it may be both. For example, when a teacher asks a student to come to the front of the class to present a paper, the student's response might consist of moving from his/her seat to the front of the class (an overt response) while at the same time experiencing a feeling of anxiety about speaking to the class (a covert response).

The receiver's response to the source's message begins the cycle of the communication process, and soon the source is responding to the receiver's feedback in some manner. Now the source's thoughts and actions are being determined by the receiver's feedback to the source's message.

THE ROLE OF NOISE IN THE COMMUNICATION PROCESS

Throughout the communication process the element *noise* can intervene and disrupt the process. As noted in the Shannon-Weaver model of communication, noise may interfere in the transmission and/or the reception of the message. Noise can permeate the communication process at any time. For example, you might be transmitting through a faulty channel: everyone has experienced the long distance call during which static on the channel (noise) disrupts the communication exchange.

Noise may be either external or internal to the communication source/receiver. Noise outside a classroom (external noise), for example, may affect the interaction between teachers and students. The student preparing to present his/her paper to the class may experience internal noise in the form of anxiety that could easily interfere with his/her transmission of the message. Daydreaming would be another example of internal noise that could interfere in the communication process.

As we have seen, the components in the communication process are interrelated and dependent upon one another. The next section of this chapter will view the various functions of the communication process.

FUNCTIONS OF THE COMMUNICATION PROCESS

One of the most important functions of the communication process is known as *affinity-seeking* (McCroskey and Wheeless, 1976). This is the process of establishing and maintaining positive relationships. According to Bell and Daly (1984) the "ability to evoke positive feelings is a favorably regarded and often envied skill" (p. 91). McCroskey, Richmond, and Payne (1986) suggest that "the degree to which we feel social needs for affection and inclusion often manifests itself in our attempts to get other people to like and appreciate us" (p. 175). From a series of studies on affinity-seeking, Bell and Daly were able to present a list of the strategies people use to get others to "like" them. The strategies most commonly occurring were such things as conversational rule-keeping, self-concept confirmation, eliciting other's disclosure, nonverbal immediacy, self-inclusion, listening, facilitating enjoyment, and altruism.

Researchers suggest that affinity-seeking communication behaviors occur in a variety of communication situations. For example, people must use their communication skills to establish and maintain positive feelings in friendships, supervisor-subordinate relationships, teacher-student relationships, and most other relationships (Bell and Daly, 1984; Richmond, McCroskey, and Davis, 1986; Richmond, Gorham, and Furio, 1987). Affinity-seeking communication behaviors usually result in increased liking and affinity, which in turn improves the communication between persons.

Another function of the communication process is known as the *information and understanding function* (McCroskey and Wheeless, 1976). We are constantly sending and receiving information and interpreting the information. This function of communication enables us to grow, learn, and adapt ourselves and our messages to the world around us. As we process information and understand information, we enable ourselves to react to the world around us and improve our communication skills. This book and other textbooks are devoted largely to this function, with a main goal of informing their readers.

Another important function of the communication process is *influence* (McCroskey and Wheeless, 1976). This function is concerned with communicating to change people's ideas, beliefs, and attitudes and perhaps get them to adopt a behavioral change. This function is usually considered successful only if the change the source seeks in the receiver takes place. If the receiver does not change his/her behavior or thinking, then the source has not been successful. For example, a teacher might be able to keep students from cheating on an exam by physically standing over them and watching them, but this type of communication is not likely to effect a change in the students' overall feeling/thinking about cheating— if getting the students to be honest in the future was the goal, the communication was unsuccessful.

Being able to process and evaluate information and participate in the *decision-making* function of communication is a needed skill (McCroskey and Wheeless, 1976). It is essential for all of us to make decisions, and often

Internal or external noise can impact the interaction between students and teachers.
WVU Photographic Services

we need to communicate with others to do so. Likewise, it is important for us to be able to assist others in making decisions about issues or things that could impact their lives, as when parents want to be able to assist their children in making decisions.

The last function of the communication process is the *confirmation* of whether or not you made the correct decision about a new idea, practice, philosophy, or product (McCroskey and Wheeless, 1976). After we have made a decision or change, we either confirm or disconfirm our decision by seeking information to support our decision. For example, one of the1 authors of this text purchased a car that is considered quite sporty without first seeking details concerning the durability and reliability of the car. To confirm that she had made a wise purchase decision, she then spent several months talking with people who had similar kinds of cars, listening to the positive things they had to say about their cars (e.g., good gas mileage, durable). If we find information supporting our decision, then we are likely to stay with our original decision, although this does not preclude us from changing our minds in the future if information is acquired later that contradicts our original decision.

In summary, the functions of communication are the very reasons we communicate with others. We want others to like us, we want to understand the world around us, we want to influence others, we want to make effective decisions, and we want to be able to validate our decisions. However, no matter how precise we are in our communication, there will always be variables that confound the communication process. The next chapter will discuss misconceptions about communication—misconceptions that may lead to ineffective communication between people.

CHAPTER

2

Misconceptions about Communication

Perhaps at one time or another you have been introduced to an individual from another part of the world— a region about which you have heard a lot but have never visited? You probably had many preconceived ideas about the person, her/his likes, dislikes, attitudes, behaviors, and so on. If your experience was like most, as your relationship with the other person progressed you began to realize many of your earlier conceptions had been inaccurate or misleading. Our relationships with other people are often like that.

When we begin study in a new area, it is somewhat like meeting a new person. We may know (or think we know) something about that area. But after we have studied in the area for a while, we may realize some of our earlier conceptions were inaccurate or misleading. If we correct those assumptions, there will be no problem. If we don't, we may have problems in that area for years to come.

The field of communication is one about which most people know some things before they begin to study it formally. Unfortunately, most people in the general population have misconceptions about the communication process and how it works. These misconceptions often lead to very ineffective communication; they may also interfere with one's learning about communication. Let's look at some of the most common conceptions about communication and consider why communication scholars believe they are *mis*conceptions.

The misconception that Interpersonal Communication is the same as intimate communication. People in this culture tend to assume that interpersonal communication and intimate communication are the same process and that communicating interpersonally means communicating in an intimate fashion. Intimate communication involves communication with another in which you discuss very private, very personal bits of information. In intimate communication you are communicating intimate details about yourself or hearing very intimate details about another. In a lifetime, most people know only three or four people with whom they feel totally comfortable and to whom they can divulge intimate details and not worry about what the other will think or do with the information. Most of our communication is of an interpersonal nature, asking a clerk in a store about the new products, asking the time from a passerby on the street, conversing with another person about the state of affairs in Iran. Very little communication on a daily basis is of a truly intimate nature. However, all intimate communication is of an interpersonal nature.

The people with whom one person is intimate may not be the same people with whom another is intimate. For example, many people will disclose intimate information to their parents or one parent, while others will not. This doesn't mean those in the latter category don't have a close relationship with their parents, it simply means they don't communicate with them about intimate details. In marital dyads, sometimes one partner feels the other partner is not communicating as many intimate details as they should to the other. Unfortunately, many marriages are doomed to failure from the beginning because of the expectations one partner may have regarding such intimacy, since in fact many people simply do not feel comfortable discussing intimate details of their lives.

Most interactions in the work environment are of an interpersonal and not intimate nature. Indeed, listeners in a work place might feel uncomfortable if a colleague consistently disclosed intimate bits of information about her/himself. People listening to this type of communication are likely to feel they should respond in a similar manner, which may begin an irreversible and undesirable cycle. The work environment is probably not the place for intimate communication, but it *is* the place for large amounts of interpersonal communication.

To aid in the understanding of how people become confused about the difference between intimate and interpersonal, let's discuss the three levels of communication (Miller and Steinberg, 1975). We can communicate at a cultural, a sociological, or a psychological level. The *cultural* level of communication is when we communicate with one another based upon cultural expectations and norms. One way to learn about cultural norms and rituals is to communicate with people from various cultures. If we cannot physically communicate with people from cultures different from our own, we can at least read about their cultures and make predictions about their communication. Cultural communication can be successful if we understand and know the culture well. However, if our predictions do not match the cultural norms, then our communication probably will be unsuccessful.

The *sociological* level of communication is determined by a person's association with groups or clubs. For example, we might wish to communicate with someone who is a member of the "group" we call high school students. If we know further that this person is a member of a honors club and the chess club, we can make additional predictions about how to communication with him/her. Groups are similar to cultures in that they have norms and rituals to which the members conform. Effective communication at the sociological level requires that we make accurate predictions of similarities among persons and we adapt our messages to those persons.

Most of us rarely communicate with others on an intimate level, but spend a lot of time communicating with others on an interpersonal level. WUV Photographic Services

The *psychological* level of communication involves adapting our communication to the unique attributes of the receiver. In order to do this we must have direct, and often personal, contact with the receiver. McCroskey, Richmond, and Stewart (1986) suggest this level is the only level at which intimate communication can occur because intimate communication involves knowing each other through revealing to the other private and personal information. They further suggest that reaching the psychological level often is possible only after we have recognized and shared with each other our cultural and social similarities. It is for this reason that not all interpersonal communication is intimate—intimacy follows after we have shared, through other levels of interpersonal communication, our broader and more basic common views, beliefs, attitudes, and so on.

Thus, the accurate statement is that some interpersonal communication is intimate, while most is not. We rarely communicate with others on an intimate level, but we spend a lot of time communicating interpersonally.

The misconception that meanings are in the words themselves. This is probably the most common misconception about communication. Though people tend to assign the "meaning" to the word, in fact the meaning resides in the mind of the person sending the message and in the mind of the person receiving the message—in their *interpretation* of the words. The sender and the receiver may or may not have the same meaning in mind when they hear a word such as "love," for instance. As communicators we try to use a common code or language to communicate with others. By its very nature, however, a language is symbolic, and each of us will interpret the symbols according to our personal and cultural background.

As an example of cross-cultural confusion inspired by meaning, several years ago the Pepsi Company had to cancel its Taiwan billboard campaign because its English slogan "Come Alive with the Pepsi Generation" was interpreted by the Taiwanese people as meaning "Pepsi will bring your ancestors back from the dead." Differing perceptions and interpretations within our own culture may be more subtle than this, but the extent to which they can affect communication should not be underestimated.

The misconception that communication is solely a verbal process. Many people assume that the term *communication* refers exclusively to the process of talking and writing. In fact, a significant portion of our communication is of a *nonverbal* form (gestures, facial expressions, and so on). Researchers suggest that anywhere from 65 to 93 percent of the meanings stimulated in the communication process are produced by some nonverbal component. This is not to suggest that verbal messages are less important than verbal, but rather illustrates the dual nature of communication. Nonverbal messages are most associated with affect or emotion, while verbal

Communication is an ongoing, nonstatic process.

Ed Petrosky, WVU Photographic Services

messages are associated with ideational content (Richmond, McCroskey, and Payne, 1987).

The misconception that to "tell" is to communicate. People sometimes assume that telling or informing someone of something represents effective communication. If this were true, people would only have to be told once how to do their jobs, how to make a bed, what to study for an exam, how to drive a car, and so on. Communicating with someone involves much more than just telling. You must be able to adapt the message to the receiver and respond to the receiver's feedback. Individuals who operate with the belief that telling is communicating are failing to recognize the active role of the receiver in the communication process. They are likely to be ineffective and insensitive communicators, unsuccessful at many of the functions of communication.

The more acceptable statement is that telling is only a part of communicating. People must be sensitive to the kinds of messages they are transmitting, both verbal and nonverbal, and their potential impact on the receiver(s). Although the meanings that receivers may assign to our messages may not be the meanings we intended to convey to them, we certainly have less reason to expect to achieve shared meaning by telling alone.

The misconception that communication will solve all our problems. We would all like to believe that simply by communicating with one another we would be able to resolve all conflict. We might think, for example, that if only the Iranian government and the United States government would get together and talk out their problems, then all conflicts would be solved. In all likelihood this is a fallacy since the two countries clearly disagree on values and issues and will probably never agree; in such a case communicating might actually do more harm than good. In fact, ineffective communication may create more problems or make present problems worse than if no communication were attempted. Effective communicators know when communication will solve and when it will create problems; they know that it is possible to "overcommunicate" about an issue and resolve nothing. It is more realistic, then, to see communication as a *catalyst* that can create problems or help solve them.

The misconception that communication is always a good thing. If you go to any region in the United States and ask passersby if communication is a good thing, the overwhelming majority will respond with a firm "yes." As we have already noted, communication will not solve all problems and in fact might create some. Hence, it is obvious that communication is not always a good thing.

Communication is neither good nor bad. It is a tool, and as with any other tool, we can abuse it or misuse it on occasions. If we use a hammer to pound in a nail, most would agree it is a good thing. However, if we use it to break the glass out of our neighbor's window, most would agree it is a bad thing. Our use of the tool determines its goodness or badness. The same is true for communication—how we use it determines its quality. We are in control of our communication just as we are in control of our hammers.

The misconception that the more communication, the better. More communication is not always better—it is the quality of the communication that is important. However, certain norms in the American culture dictate to us that the more a person talks (up to a point), the more positively he or she will be perceived by others. It is a sad fact, but a confirmed one, that in this culture talkative people are perceived as more competent, more attractive, more likely to be a leader, more powerful, and more friendly than less talkative people. Nevertheless, "the more communication, the better" is a misconception. While more may be better in many endeavors, this is not always the case with communication. We would all agree that receiving more junk mail, more memos, more talk from a person we do not like, more stinging criticism from another is certainly not "better" than receiving less of these.

People tend to equate quantity of talk with quality of talk, though it is not how much people communicate but what they communicate that is essential. Nonetheless, there are people in our culture who rarely communicate with others and are perceived negatively for their lack of communication. An even bigger problem for some of these people, when they do communicate, is that their communication is ineffective or irrelevant. This is probably due to inexperience with the communication process. These people will be discussed more thoroughly in later chapters.

The misconception that communication can break down. Someone having a problem communicating with another person may tend to blame it on a communication breakdown. Communication is an on-going, non-static process. Human communication does not break down or stop. However, it might be ineffective. "Breakdown" is a nice way of suggesting that the communication itself was ineffective—almost as if they are blaming the tool that they misuse—when in fact the sender and receiver may simply be ineffective, poor communicators.

We need to remember that human communication does not break down like some norms of technology. It is simply ineffective. *One cannot not communicate.* This means that even if we stop talking we are still communicating because our nonverbal behaviors are sending out cues to others. Many people like to use the "silent treatment" on others when they don't want to verbalize their feelings. However, the recipient of the "silent treatment" is interpreting the message of silence; hence, communication has not stopped, it is simply being transmitted by a different channel.

The misconception that communication is a natural human ability. There are no natural communicators born, just as there are no natural scientists born. However, we are born with the potential (capability) to be an effective communicator. We learn and acquire our culture's communication skills, just as we learn and acquire our culture's social skills and manners. For example, did you just naturally learn not to belch in public? Or can you remember your parents at some point telling you not to belch in public? We learn social skills by observing, modeling, being reinforced for the appropriate behaviors, and by trial and error. Some of us learn more and better than others. The same is true for communication.

Thus, communication is not a natural ability, it is learned. Most of us are born with the potential to learn communication; whether or not we acquire *effective* communication skills is up to us. Through careful instruction, personal observation, experience, and practice an individual can learn many of the communication skills needed to be a better communicator.

The misconception that communication competence equals communication effectiveness. Competence cannot be equated with effectiveness. There are speakers the world over who are competent but not effective (for example, the boring college professor who knows the subject thoroughly but bores his/her students while communicating it). Adolph Hitler is an example of a very competent communicator who was also very effective. This of course does not mean he was a good person, but he was very effective at getting people to do what he wanted them to do. A speaker may also be a very good, effective speaker without being "competent." For example, someone may deliver a very moving and persuasive speech while not being informed about the issue.

If a person possesses a great amount of knowledge about a subject matter, then he/she has a chance of being perceived as competent but may or may not be perceived as effective. Remember, a competent communicator could have a bad day and be perceived as ineffective, and an incompetent communicator could have a good day and be perceived as effective. Hence, communication competence cannot be equated with communication effectiveness, although the competent communicators have the better chance of being perceived of as effective.

One of the basic reasons underlying misunderstanding in interpersonal relationships is that people have misconceptions about what communication is or is not, and about how it functions. The purpose of this chapter was to pinpoint and assess ten of the most common communication misconceptions. The next chapter examines factors that have profound bearing on a person's ability to communicate effectively and competently and on how we perceive the communication effectiveness and competence of others.

CHAPTER

3

Shyness: The Behavior of Not Communicating

In Chapter 1 we reviewed the functions of communication and how each function works. The remaining chapters will discuss one of the most elusive, least observable phenomena with respect to communication—the way that people differ with respect to their desire for communication. It has been said that humans are social creatures, but this is only partially true. For a substantial portion of the population, being social and communicating with others is very unrewarding. In fact, it is punishing.

People with a high desire to communicate will attempt more communication and often will work hard to make that communication effective. People with a low desire to communicate will make far fewer attempts, and often will not be concerned about whether or not those attempts lead to successful communication. From this, we can infer that those people who have a low desire to communicate will be less successful at using and achieving the functions of communication. This means the people with a low desire to communicate will be less successful at affinity-seeking, gaining information and understanding, influencing others, making decisions, and confirming those decisions than those people with a high desire to communicate. Consequently, those with a low desire to communicate will fare less well in social, work, and school relationships than those with a high desire to communicate. The remainder of this chapter will review the major outcome of a low desire to communicate—shyness.

INDIVIDUAL DIFFERENCES IN COMMUNICATION

Much is made of the "uniqueness" of individual human beings. Indeed, no two human beings are exactly alike, not even identical twins. The number of ways people can differ from one another probably is infinite, but one of the more meaningful of these ways involves our patterns of communication. Many of our everyday references to people in our environment indicate our general awareness of such differences. Have you ever heard such comments as the following? "She is very quiet." "He seldom speaks up." "He never shuts up." "He has an opinion about everything and everyone." "She's a real gossip." "He always has something intelligent to say." "Getting an opinion out of him is like pulling teeth." "He's a real blow-hard." All of these comments have one thing in common—they refer to presumed habitual communication patterns of individuals that mark them as different from some (or many) other individuals. The comments differ from each other in that they refer to a variety of individual differences. The three most important types of differences fall into the categories of (1) effectiveness of communication, (2) amount of communication, and (3) desire for communication.

Effectiveness of Communication

All of us recognize that some people are far more effective communicators than are others. The successful salesperson, minister, politician, teacher, and manager are all obvious examples of effective communicators. Their opposite numbers are equally recognizable. There is a continuum that ranges from very effective communicators to very ineffective communicators with a large portion of the population being in the middle. Those in the middle envy the very effective communicators and thank their lucky stars they are not like the people at the opposite end of the continuum.

Amount of Communication

Although differences among people in terms of effectiveness are often easily recognizable, differences in the amount a person communicates (the number of times a person talks and the number of words said) are somewhat less obvious. You have probably noticed some of the following types of communicators: (1) the person who might be referred to as the "wall flower" at social gatherings who when approached seems to want to get away; (2) the person in class who always has his hand raised to answer the question; (3) the person who always has a friend or relative speak for her; (4) the person who would rather stay at home or in his room than join in social gatherings; (5) the person who avoids high interaction areas in restaurants and clubs, who would rather sit in the quiet corner; (6) the person who seems to be talking all the time, regardless of the situation; (7) the person who always has an answer for everything; (8) the teacher who assigns group work, oral reports, and so on so he/she doesn't have to talk; and (9) the supervisor who rarely meets with her/his subordinates or tries to help them solve work-related problems.

From the above list we can discern that there is a wide variety of communication behavior. Some of the differences can be accounted for by recognizing that as individuals we may talk more one day than another or in one situation than another. However, some of us talk more across virtually all situations, and some of us talk less across those same situations. In otherwords, we all fall somewhere on a continuum that goes from "talks a lot in general" to "seldom talks." Many of us fall in the middle of the continuum and whether we talk or not is determined completely by the situation. However, at the extreme ends of the continuum, there are people who will talk a lot, regardless of the situation, and there are people who will seldom talk, regardless of the situation.

Desire for Communication

As suggested earlier, the desire to communicate differs from one person to another. Desire is something that is within us and can only be inferred by another person. Some people have a great desire to communicate with other people, while some would be just as happy (or even happier) if they never had to communicate with another person. Desire for communication can be found on a continuum that goes from great desire to communicate with others to little desire to communicate with others. Many of us fall in the middle and whether we desire to communicate or not is determined by the situation. However, at the extreme ends of the continuum, there are people who have a desire to communicate a lot and there are people who have a desire to communicate as little as possible.

Desire is not as easy to tap or measure through observing behavior as effectiveness or amount of communication. We can measure effectiveness by deciding in advance what is an effective communicator in a given context and determining how closely an individual comes to meeting that criterion. We can measure amount by counting how long people talk and how many words they use. Desire is an internal state that can only be measured behaviorally by such indicants as withdrawing from communication with others, telling others you don't want to talk to them, avoiding potential communication situations, and generally acting shy. Such measures are quite imprecise. Consequently, desire can best be measured by self-report scales. We will consider some of these later.

In conclusion, it is clear from the above discussion that individual differences in communication do exist and they impact how we communicate and how others might perceive us. For example, the employee who seldom interacts with his/her peers, seldom asks questions in meetings, seldom goes to social functions, and rarely responds to the supervisor's questions may be perceived negatively by the supervisor as slow, unreliable, noncaring, or perhaps even as a trouble-maker. Hence, the individual differences in communication can determine how others will perceive you and react to you. The next section of this chapter will review the effects of individual differences with respect to communication.

EFFECTS OF INDIVIDUAL DIFFERENCES

In the North American culture, it is a well-known "fact" that there are a lot of people who "talk too much." It is also a well-known "fact" that women talk a lot more than men, and generally talk too much. These are two commonly accepted "facts" that have one thing in common—they are cultural truisms with no basis in fact. First, extensive research has been unable to discover any general differences between men and women in terms of either amount of talk or level of shyness. Some women talk more than others, so do some men. Some men talk less than others, so do some women. Second, extensive research has indicated the more a person talks, the more positively they are evaluated, other things being equal. What this indicates is that it is not an excessive *amount* of talking that causes people to have negative reactions, it is the quality of the content. For example, if someone is constantly talking about what a good student you are, or what a good employee you are, you do not become upset with this amount of talk. On the other hand, if someone is constantly talking about what a good student he/she is or what a good employee he/she is, you may become upset with this amount of talk. Hence, it is the quality and not the quantity of talk that is important in determining how others feel about talk.

The grain of truth in the truism that there are a lot of people who "talk too much" is that we tend to notice and ascribe negative perceptions to people who talk a lot but have little worthwhile to say. The grain of truth in the truism about women talking too much comes from the chauvinistic assumption that women are inferior and thus have little to contribute. The key point to remember is that in the North American culture, talk is highly valued. As a result, people in this culture have a shared stereotype that the person (man or woman) who talks more is worth more. Only when that stereotype is seriously violated by low quality of contribution are we willing to set the stereotypes aside and attribute the perception of "talks too much" to a person. But remember, in a chauvinistic environment it is much easier for a woman to violate the stereotype than it is for a man.

In general, as a person's habitual level of talk increases, the person is perceived more positively. As a person's habitual level of talk decreases, the person is perceived less positively. Clearly, then, in the North American culture, shyness is not a virtue. Most shy people clearly recognize this. Only between 10 and 20 percent of these people consider their shyness not to be a problem, the rest consider their shyness a handicap.

The majority of research efforts in the areas of verbal behavior, communication avoidance, and shyness has focused on people in the general North American culture. Virtually no research has been conducted in most other cultures. However, enough research has been reported in some cultures to indicate that the North American orientation is not at all unique. The stereotype of "the more talk the better" has also been found to be prevalent in England, Chile, and Mexico. Similarly, the proportion of shy people found in North America has been found to be essentially the same as that in Germany, Mexico, and Taiwan. However, the proportion of shy people in Puerto Rico, Israel and among American Jews is substantially lower. In most instances there have been no observed differences between men and women. However, some exceptions have been noted. The exceptions include Japan (more men than women report being shy) and Israel, Mexico, and Germany (more women than men report being shy).

No two human beings communicate exactly alike.   WVU Photographic Services

It seems that the amount of talk tends to generate comparable perceptions across most cultures—the more the better, the less the worse. The obvious conclusion one can draw from all of this is that all we have to do to be perceived more positively is to talk more. While if other things are equal, that might be true, other things seldom are equal. As we have stressed, the element that interferes with this pat answer is quality of communication. While it is true that people who talk a lot are perceived to have higher quality communication in many instances, there is also some truth to the old saying, "Keep quiet and let people think you are a fool, open your mouth and prove them right." The reason there is not a perfect correlation between the amount of talk and positive perceptions is that some very verbal people have little to say. The more they talk, the worse they look.

In conclusion, for highly verbal people with little to say, reducing the talk level may increase positive perceptions. For lowly verbal people, the picture is crystal clear—increased talk is the only path to more positive perceptions. It is not the quality of communication that is their problem, it is the amount.

NATURE OF SHYNESS

When Philip Zimbardo (1977) and his associates proposed the following two questions to over 5,000 people, they found that over 40 percent (2,000) of the people surveyed responded "Yes" to the first question and over 80 percent (4,000) responded "Yes" to one of the two questions. The questions were: Do you presently consider yourself to be a shy person? ____ Yes ____No. If you answered "No," was there ever a period in your life during which you considered yourself to be a shy person? ____Yes ____No. The results to the above are somewhat remarkable. Projecting the results of this survey nationwide, the results indicate that two out of every five people you meet consider themselves to be shy, and two more believe that they were shy at one time. Let's bring this closer to home. If there are 25 people at work, at least ten of them think of themselves as shy people. One of these could be you or your supervisor.

Now that we have an idea of how many people in our country, on a percentage basis, consider themselves to be shy, what exactly is shyness? Defining shyness has not been an easy task for writers and scholars. Zimbardo himself has said "shyness is a fuzzy concept," meaning that shyness is too vague a concept on which to pin on a single concrete definition. Pilkonis, a former student of Zimbardo's, has offered a behavioral description of shy people. He suggests that shy people are "characterized by avoidance of social interaction, and when this is impossible, by inhibition and an inability to respond in an engaging way; they are reluctant to talk, to make eye contact, to gesture, and to smile" (Pilkonis, Heape, and Klein, 1980). Buss (1984) said "shyness may be defined as discomfort, inhibition, and awkwardness in social situations, especially with people who are not familiar" (p. 39). He suggests that it is the absence of instrumental activity that identifies shyness. When someone is shy, he/she usually exhibit behaviors such as "withdrawal, reticence, and inhibition" (p. 39). He goes on to state that, "When we are shy, we tend to remain on the fringe of a conversational group, do not speak up, mumble minimal replies if addressed, and in general fail to hold up our end of the social interaction" (p. 39). He also suggests that the reaction might be so acute as to cause "shaking of the limbs, clumsy gestures, and stuttering" (p. 39). Do the above descriptions fit anyone you know?

Shy people tend to be uncomfortable in the presence of others, to be easily frightened in social situations, and to talk significantly less than nonshy people. Even if you are not a shy person yourself, you certainly know people who are. It is clear from the above that people differ greatly from one another in their typical communication behaviors and that by looking at behaviors we might be able to tell a shy person from a nonshy person. However, before we discuss types of shyness, we need to look at causes of shyness.

CAUSES OF SHYNESS

As discussed earlier, the amount of communication people engage in differs greatly from one person to another: there are people who talk constantly, regardless of the situation and then there are those who seldom talk. Those in the latter category are the people who are usually labeled as shy. There are several reasons why a person might be shy, and the reasons may vary from person to person. The following reasons seem to be the predominant ones: (1) heredity; (2) modeling; (3) childhood reinforcement; and (4) expectancy learning.

Heredity

You can look at your parents and see where you inherited such traits as height, tendency toward weight gain or slimness, color of eyes, hair color, and so on. However, you may not be able to pinpoint where you got other traitlike qualities, such as your tendency to talk a lot or little, your tendency to engage in social interaction or to avoid it. Until recently, heredity was discounted as a possible cause for differences in communication behavior and communication orientations. One only needed to point to major differences between siblings to suggest that heredity was not a credible explanation. In fact, no gene has been isolated that carries the "communication trait." However, scholars are much less willing to disregard the role of heredity today than they once were, and some are even willing to argue that heredity may be the single most important predictor of communication orientations. Some people seem to be born talkers while others are not.

Recently, researchers in the area of social biology have established that significant social traits can be measured in infants shortly after birth, and that infants differ sharply from each other on those traits. For example, infant "sociability," believed to be a predisposition directly related to adult sociability—the degree to which people reach out to other people and respond positively to contact with others—can be measured only a few weeks after birth. Other scholars have suggested that the extroversion—introversion orientation of an individual is an inherited trait and determines the orientation one has toward communication.

Research with identical twins and fraternal twins of the same sex reinforces this theoretical role of heredity. Identical twins are biologically identical, whereas fraternal twins are not. Thus, if differences between twins raised in the same environment are found to exist, biology can be discounted as a cause in one case but not the other. Actual research has indicated that biologically identical twins are much more similar in sociability than are fraternal twins. These research findings would be interesting if they were based on twin infants only, but they are even more interesting because research was conducted on a large sample of adult twins who had the opportunity to have many different and varied social experiences.

Researchers have argued for years over the impact of heredity on establishing individual differences in communication behavior and orientations. The issue is far from settled. We cannot discount the fact that heredity does give us predispositions toward communication. However, predispositions can be changed by the environment that surrounds us. Thus, while heredity probably makes a contribution to the development of communication orientations like shyness, it is only one explanation.

Modeling

Nonverbal communication researchers are positing that many of our acquired nonverbal behaviors actually come from modeling our parents, peers, and significant others. For example, little boys tend to walk much more like their fathers than like their mothers while little girls tend to walk

Many people desire to communicate with others and recognize the importance of doing so.   WVU Photographic Services

more like their mothers than their fathers. The modeling tendency has been found in children as young as three to four years of age. Researchers suggest that parents see their children modeling their behavior and then reinforce it. As a result the child continues the behavior.

Little research has been completed regarding the modeling of communication behaviors, but there does seem to be evidence that children observe the communication behaviors of their parents, peers, and significant others in their environment and attempt to emulate it. This certainly helps to explain why children who grow up in southern West Virginia have acquired the southern Appalachian accent as opposed to the New York nasal accent. It seems that both general verbal and nonverbal behaviors are influenced by modeling.

If parents are low verbalizers, then the child may learn this as the appropriate model and emulate it. If the same child enters grade school and finds that the majority of his/her elementary teachers are quiet types, then the model is reinforced and the pattern may be set for life. There is some research to suggest that children in lower grades who are exposed to teachers who are low verbalizers may become less verbal themselves.

As suggested earlier, there is reason to believe that no one explanation is responsible for the development of communication orientations and behaviors. However, it is probable that modeling, and to an even greater degree modeling in conjunction with reinforcement, makes a contribution.

Childhood Reinforcement

For years the theory of reinforcement has been the most popular explanation for behavior development and continuance. The basic premise of reinforcement is that behavior that is reinforced will increase and behavior that is not reinforced will decline. Hence, if our communication is reinforced, then we will communicate more; if our communication is not reinforced, we will communicate less.

Of the three explanations we have examined so far, this is the only one that can claim to explain why children in the same family can be almost opposite one another in terms of their communication behaviors and orientations. Since parents, teachers, siblings, and peers reinforce each child very differently, even within the same family, one child may be reinforced for communicating while another child is not reinforced for the same behavior.

In addition, most of the clinical therapy used to help people change their communication behaviors and orientations is based on reinforcement theory. The high degree of success obtained with reinforcement methods provides a strong argument in favor of this theoretical explanation.

Expectancy Learning

Much of the work in expectancy learning and its impact on communication orientations and behaviors is fairly recent, and thus research support for it is still forthcoming. The theory suggests that we seek to learn what consequences are likely to occur as a function of our behaviors (what to expect) and then try to adapt our behaviors in such a way that we increase positive outcomes and avoid negative outcomes. Hence, if we learn that the more we talk, the more someone likes us and rewards us, the more likely we are to increase our talking behavior. Through the same process we learn what we should and should not say in specific situations. Thus, we learn what to expect under each of several options open to us: not to talk, to say A, to say B, to say C, and so on. In other words, a person makes his/her behavioral choice on the basis of expectations.

Related to this explanation in a significant way is the phenomenon called "learned helplessness." In most areas of learning, over time we can develop solid expectations that are continually reinforced. In other areas we are unable to do this. Research with laboratory animals has indicated that when animals are confronted with such situations they become helpless and do nothing.

It is quite possible that in the area of communication some people confront situations like those of the laboratory animals, and so do nothing. No matter what they say, they cannot learn to predict the reactions of other people in their environment; hence, they do not communicate unless they absolutely have to. Much of this learned helplessness is created by an inconsistent reinforcement pattern. For example, at times a person may be reinforced for communicating A and at other times punished for communicating A, or a person is sometimes reinforced for talking and at other times is punished for talking.

Children and adults alike may often be unable to sort out the situational differences that produce different responses from others even though their own behaviors are the same. Hence, they become helpless and the only solution for them is to withdraw from communication. Such withdrawal is characteristic of the highly shy person, and such people often report feeling helpless in communicative situations. It is quite possible, then, that expectancy learning and reinforcement function together to produce the shy person. When expectations are learned, it is a result of consistent reinforcement patterns. When reinforcement patterns are inconsistent and unpredictable, expectancies are not learned, and helplessness followed by communication withdrawal is the consequence.

TYPES OF SHY PEOPLE

We have already noted that there may be various explanations as to why people are shy. There are several types of shy people and each is distinctly different from the others. However, they all share the common characteristic of the shy person—they don't verbalize much or often.

Skill Deficient

It seems that everyone has a least one or two areas in which they are skill deficient. For example, some people will never be great athletes. In fact they may never be even mediocre athletes and may always be poor athletes. There are also people who will never be good typists, mathematicians, cooks, and so on. All of the above have one thing in common: they never learned the skills necessary to be good at math, sports, and so on. Hence, because they know they are skill deficient, they have learned to avoid situations that show others they are skill deficient.

The same principle applies to communication. People who have poor skills in communicating with others may learn to avoid most communication situations. They may or may not make a *conscious* decision to avoid communicative situations—the behavior simply becomes a pattern. For example, a significant number of people in our society have speech problems, such as stuttering, articulation disorders, and voice problems. Not all such people become low verbalizers, but many do. Similarly, people who do not speak English as their native language (e.g., the foreign student who learned English from a foreign English teacher) are very likely to become low verbalizers in situations that require speaking English. Likewise, many talkative Americans find that they become low talkers when they travel in Europe among people who do not speak English.

In conclusion, many people become low verbalizers not because of a lack of desire to communicate, but because they lack the skills. If their skills could be improved, their communication attempts might increase.

Social Introvert

One of the most heavily researched areas in the field of personality is that of extroversion/introversion. It has been demonstrated that people differ drastically in the degree to which they wish to be with other people. Some people have a very high need and desire to be with other people (social extroverts), while others prefer to be alone most of the time (social introverts). The latter group will tend to be low verbalizers, not because of a lack of communication skills, but simply because they perceive little need for interaction.

Even though the social introvert is only one of the types of low verbalizers, it is interesting to note that people tend to perceive all low verbalizers as introverts and all high verbalizers as extroverts. This in itself causes us to misperceive people in many cases, most notably people in the public media whose job it is to be high verbalizers. Both Johnny Carson and Barbara Walters are seen by most TV viewers to be outgoing, extroverted people and yet both consider themselves to be somewhat shy and introverted.

Socially Alienated

Most people in any society attempt to conform to the norms and values of that society. This behavior is considered a sign of the "well-adjusted" person. Some individuals, however, are alienated from the society in which they live. They reject societal norms and values and may make no attempt to conform to them, becoming alienated from others.

One of the norms in most societies is that of a moderate to high amount of communication. The society values communication in its own right and also employs communication for the achievement of other goals and values. The individual who is socially alienated may reject the value of communication and become a low talker. In addition, the person may see little social utility in communication because the person is not interested in attaining the goals and values sought by other members of the society. Such people even put a negative value on communication because they see others employing it in ways they do not approve. Such orientations typically result in a low verbalization pattern for the individual.

Ethnically/Culturally Divergent

We often tend to confuse national citizenship and culture. We think and act as if everyone in a given nation or society shares the same culture. While in some small countries this might be true, it is certainly not true in the United States. We have many ethic groups and subcultural groups. Communication norms in these various groupings vary. For example, some tend to value silence more than talk.

But even in ethnic or subcultural groups where talk is highly valued, as people from the group come to interact with people from the larger society or culture communication problems may arise: even though people share a common language, we use the different dialects and accents of our subcultures and this sets us apart from other groups. Just moving from one part of the country to another (from the hills of West Virginia to the plains of Nebraska) may present a problem. In each case, the person in the minority (whether he/she is Black, White, Hispanic, Yankee, Southerner, Texan, or whatever) may be unable to cope fully with the new communication demands he/she confronts, and thus become a low verbalizer.

The Communication Apprehensive

This category is by far the largest segment of the shy population. Communication apprehension is the fear or anxiety associated with either real or anticipated communication with another person or persons (McCroskey, 1984). Many people desire to communicate with others and recognize the importance of doing so, but are impeded by their fear or anxiety. The person who has substandard communication skills or who is either ethnically or culturally divergent may also develop communication apprehension. However, most of the people who are communication apprehensive have neither substandard skills nor are divergent from the general culture. They are simply people who are afraid to communicate.

It has been estimated that 20 percent of the general population (or one in five) suffers from communication apprehension. These results have been consistent across samples of subjects and from several subject populations (over 50,000 people surveyed). Communication apprehensive people tend to be low verbalizers. If one fears something, it is natural to avoid it or withdraw from it and this is precisely what highly communication apprehensive people tend to do. Communication apprehension is an internal, cognitive state that is centered around the fear of communicating with others. In other words, *shyness is the behavior of withdrawing from communication or avoiding it, while communication apprehension is the fear of communicating which causes the behaviors of shy people.* We will discuss communication apprehension much more fully in the next chapter. However, before we do so it is important to look at the contemporary measures of shyness. Reviewing the measures will help us distinguish shyness from communication apprehension.

MEASURES OF SHYNESS

The most widely employed approach to measurement in the areas of shyness, communication apprehension, and avoidance is that of self-report measures. There are other means of measuring, such as observing and coding live behaviors and watching videotapes of the behaviors; however, these methods tend to be very time consuming. When used in conjunction with the self-report, behavioral observation methods can be very useful, however.

The measures presented here are by no means all-inclusive of the measures of shyness, but they are the more contemporary ones and the ones with a fairly substantial research base from which to predict. As noted previously, shyness is considered to be the tendency to avoid communication and talk less. The measures presented below are not all specifically labeled measures of shyness, but this is what they appear to be measuring.

The simplest measure of shyness was developed by Zimbardo (1977) and probably is the best known measure. We noted the two items on this measure earlier. The items are: Do you presently consider yourself to be a shy person? ___Yes ___No. If you answered "No," was there ever a period in your life during which you considered yourself to be a shy person? ___Yes ___No. A third item is sometimes included to obtain additional information: If you answered "Yes" to the first question, do you consider your shyness a problem? In other words, would you rather not be shy? ___Yes ___No.

McCroskey developed a Shyness Scale (SS) (Appendix A) that was reported in an article by McCroskey, Andersen, Richmond, and Wheeless in 1981. The SS measure is a 14-item, 5-step scale with good reliability and face validity. However, the Zimbardo measure is even simpler and quicker to administer and, if only a crude measure is needed, is very useful.

Most recently, McCroskey developed a Willingness to Communicate (WTC) scale (Appendix B). The WTC is the most direct measure of desire to communicate available. This instrument measures a person's willingness to communicate in four contexts (public speaking, meetings, group discussions, and interpersonal conversation) with three types of receivers (strangers, acquaintances, and friends). Both the overall score and the subscores for the various contexts and types of receivers are highly reliable and the face validity of the instrument is strong (McCroskey and Richmond, 1987). High willingness is associated with increased frequency and amount of communication, which in turn are associated with a variety of positive communication outcomes. Low willingness is associated with decreased frequency and amount of communication, which in turn are associated with a variety of negative communication outcomes.

The Willingness to Communicate scale probably is the best measure of whether a person is willing to communicate with another person in a given interpersonal encounter currently available in the communication field and it takes only a few minutes to complete. A person's willingness to communicate plays a central role in determining that individual's communicative impact on others. Thus willingness to communicate deserves to receive a high degree of attention from communication scholars.

4

Communication Apprehension: The Fear of Communication

Perhaps more than any other single communication construct, communication apprehension (CA) has been a major concern of researchers and scholars since 1970. The reason for the intensive focus on CA is because it permeates every facet of an individual's life—school, work, friendships, and so on. This chapter will examine the types of CA, the measurement of CA, the personality correlates of CA, behaviors of high versus low communication apprehensives, and effects and causes of CA.

THE NATURE OF COMMUNICATION APPREHENSION

McCroskey (1970) originally viewed CA as "a broadly based anxiety related to oral communication." In later writings (McCroskey 1977, 1978, 1984, 1986) CA came to be defined as "an individual's level of fear or anxiety associated with either real or anticipated communication with another person or persons." The term "oral" was included in the original definition since much of the earlier work on CA was founded upon work in the areas of stage fright and reticence. Because of subsequent research that did not focus on talking, it was concluded that CA "encompasses all modes of communication" and should not be restricted to talking, although apprehension about talking is the more common form of CA (McCroskey, 1984).

It was the work of Daly and Miller (1975) in the area of writing apprehension and the work of Andersen, Andersen, and Garrison (1978) in the area of singing apprehension that spawned the rethinking of the CA construct.

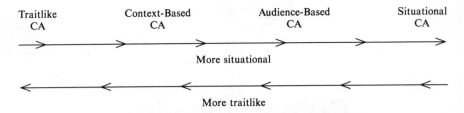

FIGURE 4. Communication Apprehension Continuum.

Both sets of researchers were former students of McCroskey. Their work with him on studies concerning CA helped generate their thinking about their constructs.

Writing Apprehension is the fear or anxiety associated with writing situations (Daly and Miller, 1975). Daly and Miller developed the Writing Apprehension Test (WAT), which is widely used in the field of English to measure a student's apprehension about writing (see Appendix C). A person's score on the WAT may range between 20 and 100. The higher the score, the more apprehension one generally feels about writing. Scores below 45 indicate a very low level of apprehension about writing. People with scores in this area are likely to enjoy writing generally and to seek opportunities to write. The range of scores between 45 and 75 represent the "normal" range of apprehension about writing. For people in this range, some writing will create apprehension while other writing will not. Scores above 75 indicate a very high level of apprehension about writing. People with such high scores will be troubled about many kinds of writing and are likely to avoid writing in most situations when they can.

The WAT has a moderate correlation (around .30) with the Personal Report of Communication Apprehension (PRCA), which focuses on oral communication apprehension. This means apprehensions about talking and writing are somewhat related. However, it also means it is quite possible for a person to be very apprehensive about one form of communication but not apprehensive about the other. The PRCA will be discussed later in this chapter.

While the singing apprehension construct did not receive as much attention in the literature as did the CA research and the WAT research, it should still be noted as a concern of communication scholars in the area of CA. Andersen, Andersen, and Garrison (1978) developed the Test of Singing Apprehension (TOSA) to measure a person's fear or anxiety about singing (see Appendix D). The TOSA was found to have a very low correlation with the PRCA. Thus, apprehension about talking and about singing appear to be generally unrelated.

In sum, the CA construct has been substantially broadened and redefined over the past decade. We will now turn to the current conceptualization of CA.

TYPES OF COMMUNICATION APPREHENSION

Based upon the research in the area of CA, it is useful to think of communication apprehension on a four-point continuum (see Figure 4). At one end of the continuum and moving to the other extreme, the four points are: (1) communication apprehension as a trait, (2) communication apprehension in a generalized context, (3) communication apprehension with a given audience across situations, and (4) communication apprehension with a given individual or group in a given situation. As McCroskey (1984) states, "this continuum can be viewed as ranging from the extreme trait pole to the extreme state pole, although neither the pure trait nor pure state probably exists as a meaningful consideration (p. 15, 16)." Each of the types of CA is discussed below.

Traitlike CA

The term *traitlike* was chosen because it indicates a distinction between an actual trait (e.g., eye color, height, weight, and so on) and something that is trait*like*. A true trait is something that is "invariant" and cannot be changed. Of course, you can disguise your eye color by wearing tinted contact lenses, but you can not change your true eye color permanently. Communication apprehension does not meet these criteria—that is, it is not a trait in the strictest sense of the term—but it *is traitlike*. Traitlike personality variables, such as CA, extroversion, and dogmatism are highly resistant to change, but this does not mean that they cannot be changed. Individuals, usually as adults, may succeed at consciously changing aspects of their personalities, but such changes are usually accomplished in conjunction with some treatment program.

Hence, traitlike CA is viewed as "a relatively enduring, personality-type orientation toward a given mode of communication across a wide variety of contexts" (McCroskey, 1984, p. 16). Most of the CA research in the 1970s concentrated on the study of traitlike CA. The measures discussed previously (PRCA, WAT, and TOSA) measure a general predisposition, a traitlike personality orientation. This assumes that a person's score on one of the measures will be similar across an extended period of time. In other words, traitlike personality orientations are expected to remain about the same, across time, unless there is some type of intervention program.

Hence, if you are generally traitlike communication apprehensive on Tuesday, you will probably be that way on Thursday of the following week and Monday of the next year, unless you have treatment for the reduction of CA. During interviews with people who have high levels of communication apprehension, we have asked, "Do you ever feel less anxious?" The answer typically is "When I am with my family or people I know very well; otherwise, I am usually anxious about communicating with others." They often comment that the interview makes them very nervous, even though we are usually well acquainted with them before we ask such questions.

The Personal Report of Communication Apprehension-24 (PRCA-24: McCroskey, 1982) is the best available measure of traitlike communication apprehension (see Appendix E). As with most personality-type measures, your PRCA-24 score can predict your behavior only if your score is extremely high or low. Such extreme scores suggest that your behavior is influenced as much, if not more, by your general feelings about communication than by the specific communication situation in which you find yourself. Either you are anxious in virtually all communication situations or you are anxious in virtually no communication situations. Scores may range from 24 to 120. Any score above 65 indicates that you are more generally apprehensive about communication than the average person. Scores above 80 indicate a very high level of traitlike CA. Scores below 50 indicate a very low level of CA. Extreme scores (below 50 or above 80) are abnormal. This means that the degree of apprehension you experience may not be associated with a realistic response to a situation. For example, people with very low scores may not experience apprehension in situations in which they should, and people with very high scores might experience apprehension in situations where there is no rational reason for such anxiety.

As noted earlier, about 20 percent of the population falls in each extreme category. It is important to clarify the meaning we are assigning to the terms low and high communication apprehension. People in the so-called normal range of communication apprehension tend to respond very differently in different situations; one situation (e.g., a job interview) might prompt them to be highly anxious while another situation (e.g., answering a question in class) might result in no anxiety or tension at all. The "low" and the "high" communication apprehensive, however, tends to respond to virtually all oral communication situations in the same way. In summary, traitlike CA is an enduring orientation about communication and usually doesn't change unless there is some form of intervention.

Context-Based CA

This type of CA relates to people who are fearful or anxious about communicating in one type of context, while having no fear or anxiety in other contexts. The most common form of this is the fear of public speaking or stage fright.

Context-based CA is viewed as "a relatively enduring, personality-type orientation toward communication in a given type of context" (McCroskey, 1984, p. 16). This type of communication apprehension relates to generalized types of situations. Other examples, beside public speaking, include going on job interviews, meeting new people, and the like. The Personal Report of Public Speaking Anxiety (PRPSA: McCroskey, 1970) will determine your fear about public speaking (see Appendix F). Your score on the PRPSA can range between 34 and 170.

Scores on the PRPSA that are between 34 and 84 indicate very low anxiety about public speaking. Very few public speaking situations would produce anxiety in people whose scores are this low. Scores between 85 and 92 indicate a moderately low level of anxiety about public speaking. While some public speaking situations would be likely to arouse anxiety in people with such scores, most situations would not be anxiety arousing. Scores between 93 and 110 indicate moderate anxiety in most public speaking situations, but the level of anxiety is not likely to be so severe that the individual cannot cope with it and be a successful speaker.

Scores that range between 111 and 119 suggest a moderately high level of anxiety about public speaking. People with such scores will tend to avoid public speaking because it usually arouses a fairly high level of anxiety in them. While some public speaking situations may not cause too much of a problem, most will be very problematic. Scores between 120 and 170 indicate a very high level of anxiety about public speaking. People with scores in this range have very high anxiety in most, if not all, public speaking situations and are likely to go to considerable lengths to avoid such situations. It is unlikely that they can become successful public speakers unless they are able to overcome or significantly reduce their anxiety.

When we discussed oral communication apprehension and the PRCA-24, we noted that the "normal" range of scores included only moderate levels of CA. The picture is quite different when we look at anxiety about public speaking. Of the several thousand college students who have completed the PRPSA, the following percentages have been found in the five categories: low anxiety, 5 percent; moderately low anxiety, 5 percent; moderate anxiety, 20 percent; moderately high anxiety, 30 percent; and high anxiety, 40 percent. Thus, the "normal" range for public speaking is in the moderate to high categories, since that is where most people's scores fall. What this suggests, then, is that it is "normal" to experience a fairly high degree of anxiety about public speaking. Most people do. If you are highly anxious about public speaking, then you are "normal."

Although there is no necessary relationship between trait communication apprehension level and level of communication apprehension concerning any particular generalized context, it is much more likely that a person who is high in trait communication apprehension will have high communication apprehension in more generalized contexts. The reverse is true for the person with low trait communication apprehension.

Of particular importance here is the proportion of people who experience high communication apprehension in given generalized contexts. While only 20 percent of the population experiences high traitlike communication apprehension, estimates run as high as 80 percent of the population for generalized context communication apprehension--over 70 percent for the public speaking context alone. Thus, while such communication apprehension is very likely to make one uncomfortable and interfere with communication, it is very normal for a person to experience high communication apprehension in at least one generalized context.

McCroskey and Richmond (1980; 1982) developed measures of communication apprehension in generalized contexts (see Appendix G). To obtain a rough idea about your level of communication apprehension in generalized contexts, complete the five measures in Appendix G. By comparing your score on each of the other four scales with your general score on the scale, you can identify what kinds of situations—talking in groups, meetings, interpersonal conversations, or giving speeches—cause you to be more or less apprehensive. Any score above 30 indicates some communication apprehension about that kind of situation. Scores above 35 indicate a comparatively high level of communication apprehension about that situation.

Audience-Based CA

This type of CA is concerned with a person's reactions to communicating with a given individual or group of individuals across time. For example, some individuals and groups may cause a person to be highly apprehensive while other individuals or groups do not produce any apprehension. This type of CA is very situation specific and may not be the same from one person to another. However, almost 95 percent of the population reports having communication apprehension about communicating with some person or group in their lives. The target that may produce this apprehension may be the boss, dad, a teacher, a colleague at work, or virtually anyone else in the person's environment. It is quite normal to be apprehensive when communicating with certain individuals or groups.

Audience-based CA is viewed as "a relatively enduring orientation toward communication with a given person or group of people" (Mc-Croskey, 1984, p. 17). This type of CA is not seen as personality based, but as a response to situational constraints generated by the other person or group. Although it is not possible to predict which people will make high trait communication apprehensives most uncomfortable or low trait communication apprehensives most uncomfortable, we do know that the high trait apprehensives will have apprehension aroused in them by more people than will the low trait apprehensives. Once again, the trait of high communication apprehension is reflected in an increased probability of fear or anxiety in any given situation, but certainly not in all situations. This type of CA is produced by the situational constraints more than by the personality of the individual. Hence, length of acquaintance should be considered here. Richmond (1978) found that, while personality orientations should be expected to be somewhat predictive in the early stages of acquaintance of CA, in later stages of acquaintance the situational constraints predict more of the apprehension experienced by the individual.

Much less attention has been paid to the measurement of audience-based CA than traitlike CA. However, Spielberger (1966) developed a state anxiety measure that was later modified by Richmond (1978). The most recently developed measure of this type of CA is known as the Situational Communication Apprehension Measure (SCAM: McCroskey and Richmond, 1982. See Appendix H). Your score on this measure may range between 20 and 140.

The SCAM is designed to measure the apprehension you feel while participating in a specific communication situation or talking with a specific audience. As a result, it can be used to measure your apprehension about any given communication situation or audience, such as talking with your supervisor, your parents, giving a report in a class, going on a job interview, calling someone for a date, or something as simple as answering the phone or talking with a stranger. In this instance (Appendix H), we asked you to complete the scale with regard to how you felt in your last interaction with someone who had a supervisory position over you (e.g., a teacher if you are a student, your principal if you are a teacher, and so on). We chose this situation arbitrarily; any other situation could illustrate SCAM as well. If you are apprehensive about asking someone for a date, use this and complete the scales.

Scores on the SCAM between 20 and 50 indicate very low apprehension about the given communication situation. This is the amount of apprehension a typical person might feel while talking with a very close friend.

Scores between 70 and 90 represent a moderate amount of apprehension. A score in this range would suggest some discomfort, but not enough for a person to avoid that kind of interaction. Scores from 110 to 140 indicate a very high level of apprehension. It is quite likely that if a person feels this high a level of apprehension in a given communication situation the person will try to avoid that situation in the future. If the situation cannot be avoided, it is likely that person will be a low talker in this instance.

There is no way to estimate what is "normal" on the SCAM since it is clearly "normal" to respond to different situations differently. Thus, if you were to complete the scale on several different audiences, you should see quite a variety in your scores. Of course, people who have high scores on the PRCA-24 are likely to have high scores on the SCAM in more situations than would other people, and the reverse would be true for people with low scores on the PRCA-24.

Situational CA

At the far end of our continuum is communication apprehension that is experienced only with a given individual or group in a single situation. Virtually 100 percent of us experience this form of communication apprehension at one time or another—for example, when your teacher calls you into his office and tells you that he suspects you of cheating; when your boss calls you in and tells you she suspects you of "borrowing" company equipment; when with only five minutes notice you are expected to give a twenty-minute presentation to a group on a topic you know very little about; or when you have to go to court to testify in a murder trial.

Situational CA is viewed as "a transitory orientation toward communication with a given person or group of people" (McCroskey, 1984, p. 18). It is not viewed as personality based, but rather "as a response to the situational constraints generated by the other person or group" (McCroskey, 1984, p. 18). This type of CA will fluctuate as a function of the constraints introduced by the other person or group. Even though people with high traitlike CA and high context-based CA would be expected to experience high situational CA, knowledge of levels of neither of these should be highly predictive of which situations will produce the high CA. However, audience-based CA should be moderately highly related to situational CA. This type of CA has received little attention in terms of measurement compared to the other types. However, the SCAM can be used to satisfactorily measure situational CA (McCroskey and Richmond, 1982; McCroskey, 1984).

In conclusion, Figure 5 illustrates the four types of communication apprehension. As noted in the figure, the three components of this conceptualization are context, audience (person/group), and time. This was first

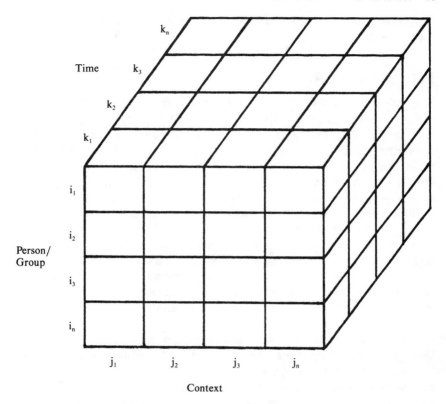

Note: Traitlike = grand sum of all $i_x j_x k_x$ cells.
Context-based = j_x across time and context.
Audience-based = i_x across time and context.
Situational = each $i_x j_x k_x$ cell.

FIGURE 5. Types of Communication Apprehension. [*Source:* From James C. McCroskey, "Oral Communication Apprehension: A Reconceptualization, " in M. Burgoon (Ed.) *Communication Yearbook 6* (Beverly Hills, CA: Sage, 1982), p. 150.]

presented by McCroskey (1984). He suggests that traitlike CA cuts across time, receiver, and situation. This is what would be expected with a personality orientation such as traitlike CA. Context-based CA is seen as "that which is associated with a single type of communication context cutting across receiver and time." Person-group CA is seen as apprehension that is "associated with a single receiver or group of receivers cutting across context and time." Situational CA is apprehension that is "specific to a given context with a given receiver at a given time" (McCroskey, 1984, p. 19).

Pathological CA

This is not necessarily a type of CA, but rather the unique person who either experiences CA when they should not or never experiences CA, even when they should. CA is an orientation that people have about communicating with others; it is not a type of person. Every individual is impacted by CA to greater or lesser extent. However, when, over time, someone behaves abnormally to threatening situations, they are considered pathological. For example, when someone withdraws from a threatening situation, this is normal; when a person does *not* withdraw from a threatening situation when she/he should, this is pathological.

Another example of pathological behavior is when a person talks excessively at inappropriate times, regardless of the circumstances surrounding the situation. Even though this person is an obvious low apprehensive, such behavior is still pathological in the sense that the individual doesn't know how to gauge appropriate communication behavior.

Several years ago we became acquainted with a faculty member in a university who would never cease talking, even when the Dean of the College had told him it was time to be quiet. Eventually, this person was asked to leave the university, largely due to his deviant, pathological behaviors about talking even when he should be listening. He was an authority on all things, regardless of their nature and his colleagues simply couldn't work with him. Hence, pathological CA can take the form of a person who talks when he/she shouldn't (e.g., the low apprehensive who is never afraid to say anything at any time) or a person who won't talk when he/she should (e.g., the high apprehensive who will not talk even when the situation is nonthreatening).

Some groups of people may appear pathological but they are not. For example, if you have ever attended a conference for top-notch salespersons, you know that they talk constantly. Remember this is their orientation—the more you talk the more you sell. Hence, this is normal communication behavior for their group. Also, keep in mind that some cultures value quietness more than talk. While people in these cultures may seem excessively quiet to us, they are nonetheless displaying normal communication behavior.

It should be clear from the above discussion of the four types of CA that a person's level of traitlike CA is very much a part of that person's overall personality. Our next section will review the personality correlates of traitlike CA.

PERSONALITY CORRELATES OF TRAITLIKE COMMUNICATION APPREHENSION

Communication apprehension is very much a part of a person's overall personality. Although no two human beings are exactly alike, if they possess similar traits and personality characteristics, one can predict how they might respond in different situations. This section will examine the personality patterns of people with high and low levels of traitlike CA. This will assist us in understanding how each type of person approaches their environment and interaction with others in their environment.

General Anxiety

General anxiety is characterized by an uneasiness and worry that goes across situations. The person with a high degree of general anxiety is uneasy and worried virtually all of the time, whether there is good reason for such concern or not. This person is likely to be restless most of the time, and to be impatient and tense.

General anxiety is often confused with communication apprehension. It is easy to understand why this confusion occurs, since people with either high communication apprehension or high general anxiety are likely to exhibit some of the same behaviors in communication situations. They may fidget, repeat themselves, get a dry mouth or get an upset stomach, and so on. The key difference is that these characteristics are common to persons with high general anxiety both in communication situations and in other situations, whereas for high communication apprehensives they only occur in communication situations. Although these two aspects of personality are not the same thing, this does not mean they are not related. People with high levels of general anxiety are more likely to be high communication apprehensives, and vice versa. Similarly, people with low levels of communication apprehension are less likely to have a high level of general anxiety. It is important to remember, however, that just because a person has a high or low level of communication apprehension, it does not necessarily follow that the person has a matching level of general anxiety.

Tolerance for Ambiguity

Some people have a personality that allows them to function in a communication environment where there is a lot of uncertainty. Other people have little or no tolerance for uncertain situations. This personality variable is known as "tolerance for ambiguity."

People with a low tolerance for ambiguity are likely to have higher levels of communication apprehension. Similarly, people with high levels of tolerance for ambiguity are likely to have lower levels of communication apprehension. When confronted with an ambiguous situation, these two types of people are likely to behave very differently: since such situations increase demands for communication, the high communication apprehensive is very likely to withdraw, whereas the low communication apprehensive is likely to increase communication. While the relationship is far from perfect, tolerance for ambiguity and communication apprehension are negatively related. As level of communication apprehension increases, tolerance for ambiguous communication decreases and the probability of withdrawal from such situations increases.

Self-Control

Self-control is the personality variable that relates to how much control a person has over her/his own emotions. Degree of self-control and communication apprehension are negatively related; as communication apprehension increases, self-control tends to decrease. As might be expected, people high in self-control tend to be more calm, more composed, more in control in general, and less afraid of communicating. People who are low in self-control are more likely to be high communication apprehensives. They are afraid to talk and communicate because they are insecure and lack control over their emotional states. They may withdraw from communication so that they do not lose control over their emotions and say things they do not mean.

Adventurousness

A person with an adventurous personality is one who enjoys new experiences and tends to become bored with routine or repetitive matters. Such people like to experience new things, people, places, and ideas. They tend to be more sociable and outgoing and have a lot of variability in their emotional responses. People low in adventurousness, on the other hand, tend to be cautious, somewhat withdrawn, and sometimes feel somewhat inferior to others around them.

Communication is one of the pathways to new experiences. Thus, adventurous individuals are less likely to have high levels of communication apprehension. They show more interest in communication and are likely to seek communication opportunities. Individuals low in adventurousness are more likely to be communication apprehensive and to withdraw from prospective communication experiences.

Emotional Maturity

Have you ever met a person who is very changeable, who is friendly and pleasant one day but out-of-sorts the next, who is easily upset and annoyed in work or social settings? This person likely is suffering from a lack of emotional maturity. A person with an emotionally mature personality tends to be stable, calm, and well balanced most of the time.

Most emotionally mature people enjoy communicating and show a much greater desire to communicate, greater flexibility in their communication, and greater adaptability to the moods of others with whom they are communicating. The more emotionally mature a person is, the less likely it is that he or she will be a high communication apprehensive. Emotionally immature people have difficulty just handling themselves without the increased pressure of relating to others. Thus, communication can become very problematic to the emotionally immature. Such people are more likely to become high communication apprehensives.

Introversion

The person with an introverted personality tends to be shy and withdrawn and prefers to spend much time alone. Generally, introverts find other people to have a very limited appeal, and they are happier when they are alone. At the other end of the personality continuum, extroverts are bold, aggressive, and talkative. They are much happier when they are with other people.

Introverts tend to have higher levels of communication apprehension. Extroverts tend to have lower levels of communication apprehension. However, this relationship is far from perfect. Some introverts have little or no apprehension about communicating; they simply prefer not to communicate because they simply do not care that much for other people. They may withdraw from communication, but they do so from preference rather than from fear. Similarly, some extroverts have fairly high levels of communication apprehension, but they are so people oriented that they force themselves to communicate in spite of their fears. Consequently, we may sometimes mistake the introvert for the high communication apprehensive or the extrovert for the low communication apprehensive. Their communication behaviors are very similar. Nevertheless, such mistakes are the exception rather than the rule. The relationship between introversion and high communication apprehension is positive and moderately strong.

Self-Esteem

Self-esteem refers to the way a person evaluates her/himself in terms of overall worth. People with low self-esteem tend to feel that they are not very worthwhile, that they are more likely to fail than to succeed, that they are less competent than other people around them. In contrast, people with high self-esteem see themselves as valuable members of society, as winners who are competent and likely to be successful.

People with low self-esteem tend to have higher levels of communication apprehension; people with high self-esteem tend to have lower communication apprehension. Those in the latter group expect to succeed in their communication experiences, just as they expect to succeed in other ways. People with high self-esteem tend to be leaders in most communication environments, while those with low self-esteem tend to be the followers.

Innovativeness

Innovativeness is the personality characteristic that refers to a person's willingness to change or accept change in the society around them. There is a strong negative relationship between an individual's innovativeness and their level of communication apprehension. High levels of innovativeness tend to be associated with low levels of communication apprehension. People who are willing to introduce a change must be willing to communicate about that change. They also must be willing to accept challenges about the usefulness of the change. This makes it very difficult for a high communication apprehensive to be very innovative. As a consequence, high communication apprehensives may become resistant to change because change tends to require increased communication within their environment.

Tolerance for Disagreement

Tolerance for disagreement is an individual's tolerance for other people taking positions different from one's own. Some people are able to tolerate a very high level of disagreement before they feel they are in conflict with another person, while others have a very low level of such tolerance. For example, competitive debaters tend to have a very high level of tolerance for disagreement because of the communication environment in which they exist. Debaters are constantly in disagreement with one another; hence in order to succeed, they must be able to handle this disagreement without taking it personally.

Tolerance for disagreement is negatively associated with communication apprehension. People with high levels of communication apprehension tend to have low levels of tolerance for disagreement. Because communication demands increase when disagreement is present, and communication is not rewarding to them, even a small amount of disagreement can cause high communication apprehensives to perceive that they are in conflict with another person. At this point, high communication apprehensives have to choose between more communication and submission to the other person. Typically, they choose to submit. High communication apprehensives, then, tend to have a low tolerance for disagreement and usually try their best to avoid situations in which disagreement is likely to occur.

Assertiveness

Assertiveness refers to the way people assert or defend themselves and their rights as individuals. People with low assertiveness tend to not be able to take up for themselves and often get taken advantage of by others. People with high levels of assertiveness tend to get ahead and not let others take advantage of them. This does not mean that they are aggressive or rude; they simply "stand their own ground."

People with high assertiveness tend to have low levels of communication apprehension. On the other hand, people with low assertiveness tend to have high levels of communication apprehension.

From the relationships between communication apprehension and other personality characteristics that have been discussed in this section, we can draw generalized profiles of the high and low communication apprehensive. The person who is highly communication apprehensive tends to suffer from general anxiety, to have a low tolerance for ambiguity, to lack self-control, to not be adventurous, to lack emotional maturity, to be introverted, to have low self-esteem, to not be innovative, to have a low tolerance for disagreement, and to not be assertive. On the other hand, the person who has a low level of communication apprehension tends to have little general anxiety, to be able to tolerate ambiguous situations, to have a high degree of self-control, to be adventurous, to be emotionally mature, to be extroverted, to have high self-esteem, to be innovative, to be able to tolerate relatively high levels of disagreement, and to be assertive.

While these profiles, based on extensive research, are accurate in general, they do not necessarily apply to any single individual with either high or low communication apprehension. As we noted at the outset of this section, no two individuals have exactly the same personalities. The profiles we have outlined are useful to understanding the *general* ways that both high and low communication apprehensives relate to other people and their environment. This picture becomes much clearer upon examination of specific behavioral differences between high and low communication apprehensives, which we will do in the following section.

BEHAVIORS OF HIGH AND LOW COMMUNICATION APPREHENSIVES

We noted previously that the main impact of communication apprehension on people's behavior is in terms of their tendency to seek or avoid communication. People with high communication apprehension tend to avoid or withdraw from situations that will require communication. People with low communication apprehension will tend to seek opportunities to communicate with other people. In this section we will review how these general tendencies influence behavior in specific situations and settings.

Classroom Setting

The classroom is a major communication environment. As such, it is not surprising that behaviors of high and low communication apprehensives in the classroom are substantially different.

To begin with, high and low communication apprehensives, when given free choice, make different decisions concerning what classes to take. Low communication apprehensives prefer classes with small enrollments where there is ample opportunity for students to interact with each other and with the instructor. High communication apprehensives, in contrast, tend to avoid such small classes in favor of larger, lecture-type classes in which most of the communication takes the form of the instructor talking to the students and the students simply listening and taking notes.

What is expected in the class in terms of communication also influences an individual's choice of classes. Classes that require oral reports or speeches are avoided by high communication apprehensives but are attractive to low communication apprehensives. Similarly, classes that base part of the final grade on "class participation" are attractive to low communication apprehensives but are disliked by those with higher apprehension.

Once a student is enrolled in a class, whether voluntarily or through a requirement, we might assume the student will simply accept the requirements with regards to communication and try to do his or her best. Such an assumption is incorrect. High communication apprehensives often will drop a class with high communication requirements, even if it is a required course. For example, one study found that over 50 percent of the students with high communication apprehension dropped a required public speaking course during the first three weeks of the course, just before the first speech was due to be presented. Other studies have found that high communication apprehensives who remain in courses with high communication requirements are very likely to be absent on days when they are scheduled for presentations. This is true not only at the college and high school levels but also at the elementary school level where "show and tell," "see and say," or "book report" assignments are required. Young children often claim they are unable to read so they can avoid having to read aloud to the class.

Low communication apprehensives are likely to engage in similar behaviors if there is little opportunity for communication in the course. Their attendance in lecture classes is likely to be low; they would rather get the necessary information by reading or talking to other students than sit through "all those lectures." Similarly, research has indicated that low communication apprehensives do not like automated, individualized instruction situations in which they are given objectives, reading or viewing assignments, and tests with no opportunity for interaction with a live

Some communication situations, such as job interviews, meeting new people, tend to make people anxious.   WVU Photographic Services

teacher. They are likely to avoid or withdraw from the class or, as an alternative if they must have the class, complete it in as short a time as possible.

Where a person chooses to sit in a classroom also reflects the person's level of communication apprehension. Low communication apprehensives tend to sit in the front and center of the traditional classroom. High communication apprehensives tend to sit along the sides and in the rear of the room. Most interaction in the typical classroom is focused on the center of the room in the first few rows. This is where the low apprehensive chooses to sit, and where the high communication apprehensive tries her/his best to avoid.

Finally, type and amount of participation in the class are both affected by communication apprehension. Low communication apprehensives frequently volunteer to participate, even if they are not certain that they know the correct answer. High communication apprehensives will almost never volunteer to participate, even if they are certain they know the correct answer. In some instances, they even will knowingly give a wrong answer when called upon because they think that will decrease their chance of being called upon at a later date. Recent research with college students demonstrated that when high CA students were told they would be asked to participate in class by recalling information given in a lecture for another classmate they lost approximately 20 percent of the information. Their recall dropped sharply in contrast to the classes in which other high CA students were not told they would have to communicate later. In other words, when the high CA college student thinks he/she will be asked to talk to a classmate and recall classroom content, the anxiety about communication interferes with their cognitive learning and later recall of what is taught (Booth-Butterfield, 1988).

In short, communication apprehension has a direct impact on student preferences for instructional systems and on student behaviors in the classroom. In most instances the tendencies of high communication apprehensives push them toward behaviors that decrease their likelihood for success in the academic setting, but the tendencies of low communication apprehensives push them toward behaviors that increase their likelihood of success.

Small Group Settings

While a small group discussion setting is less threatening to most people than is a public speaking setting, and particularly so to a person with high communication apprehension, this setting still places rather high communication demands on an individual. Consequently, it is not surprising that high communication apprehensives typically attempt to avoid small group communication or to sit rather quietly in a group if they must be present. Low communication apprehensives, of course, tend to enjoy such experiences, participate fully or even dominate the group, and frequently volunteer to serve on committees, even to chair them.

While less talk on the part of high communication apprehensives in a small group is predictable from our earlier discussions, some of the other behaviors in which high communication apprehensives have been found to engage are not as predictable. For example, not only do they talk less, they also say things that are less relevant to the on-going discussion. It appears that this behavior has been learned as a means of getting people to stop asking the high apprehensive questions. Additionally, the number of "I don't know" answers coming from high communication apprehensives is disproportionately high compared to other group members.

Finally, both low and high communication apprehensives seem to have an innate ability to figure out where to sit in a small group setting in order to either facilitate or inhibit their communication. Research has indicated that low communication apprehensives choose seats that facilitate interaction and lead to their taking on leadership function. On the other hand, high communication apprehensives choose seats that inhibit communication and denote low status and power.

Dyadic Settings

The behavior of high and low communication apprehensives in dyadic relationships (communication between two people) differs sharply, as it does in other settings. In general, low communication apprehensives assume a dominant, leadership role, while high communication apprehensives assume a submissive, follower role.

The insecurity of the high communication apprehensive is reflected by the very low amount of self-disclosure in which they engage. They prefer not to talk about themselves. Also, they seem overly concerned with being certain that the other dyad member understands or agrees with them. They use a disproportionately large number of expressions known as "rhetorical interrogatives," such as "you know?" "OK?" and "you see what I mean?" Low communication apprehensives, of course, engage in much more self-disclosure and use proportionately fewer rhetorical interrogatives.

In studies that have coded actual verbal behavior, a major difference in behavior between high and low communication apprehensives has been observed. Whereas low communication apprehensives communicate in a dominant fashion, attempting to control their dyad partner, high communication apprehensives tend to communicate in an unassertive manner.

Occupations differ greatly in the degree to which they place communication demands on an individual.   WVU Photographic Services

They seldom disagree and often submit to the assertions and requests of their dyad partner. We might speculate that this type of communication behavior is related to the high communication apprehensives low tolerance for disagreement and low assertiveness.

Social Settings

Since most social settings involve communicating in dyads or small groups, it is not surprising that high and low communication apprehensives differ in their behaviors relating to social settings. While low communication apprehensives tend to involve themselves in more social activities in general than do high communication apprehensives, the most striking differences in their social behaviors relate to dating and marriage.

Research indicates that high and low communication apprehensives have an equal desire for a social relationship with a member of the opposite sex. However, low apprehensives report having over twice as many dates in a given time period as do high communication apprehensives. However, high communication apprehensives report twice the frequency of steady dating reported by low communication apprehensives. Thus, it appears that if a high communication apprehensive is to have a social relationship with a member of the opposite sex, it will tend to be an exclusive relationship. On the other hand, low communication apprehensives appear to "play the field." The strong tendency to engage in exclusive relationships on the part of high communication apprehensives is also evident from their behavior with regard to marriage. In a study of college graduates ranging in age from 23 to 64, it was found that over 50 percent of high communication apprehensives married within a year after completing their undergraduate degree. No similar pattern was found for low communication apprehensives.

These behavioral patterns suggest that high communication apprehensives find it difficult to establish social relationships and thus make a very strong effort to maintain ones they can establish. Low communication apprehensives, on the other hand, find it easier to establish social relationships and as a result may be less likely to maintain a relationship that is not completely acceptable to them.

Occupational Choices

The choice of an occupation is one of the most significant choices an individual makes. In large measure this choice will determine whether the individual will be happy in later life, whether the individual will be successful, and what the economic and social standing of the individual will be. While many factors influence the choice of an occupation, one of the most important—and possibly the most important—is that individual's level of communication apprehension.

Occupations differ greatly in the degree to which they place communication demands on an individual. Consider the differences, for example, between the occupations of biochemist and trial lawyer, or between barber and accountant, or between forest ranger and salesperson. We certainly should not be surprised that high communication apprehensives tend to choose occupations with lower communication demands and low communication apprehensives tend to choose occupations with high communication demands. If it were otherwise, the individual might be poorly adjusted, unhappy, and unsuccessful.

However, we must not overlook an important fact. In contemporary society, both in the United States and other industrialized societies, high status and economic reward occupations, with only a very few exceptions, are also occupations with very high communication demands. In spite of this, the choices people make are those we would expect based on our knowledge of their CA level. The implications of these choices on the everyday lives of individuals will be considered in a later chapter.

Housing Choices

Where one lives can have a major impact on the amount of communication demanded of that person. Some housing areas place the individual into almost constant contact with others while others provide very little contact.

Housing choices, like occupational choices, are influenced by many factors—not the least of which are cost, location, and availability. Nevertheless, when choosing a place to live, people normally are confronted with several available choices within their financial limitations. Trying to determine the impact that communication apprehension has on housing choice might seem elusive. However, several conclusions can be drawn from the research on housing choice and its relationship to CA.

High communication apprehensives tend to choose living accommodations that inhibit incidental contact with other people, whereas low communication apprehensives tend to choose accommodations that enhance the possibilities of such contact. For example, in a college dormitory high communication apprehensives usually prefer to live at the ends of hallways, unless there is a stairway, elevator, or restroom there. Stairways, elevator waiting areas, and restrooms tend to be high interaction areas, so rooms near such areas are desirable to low communication apprehensives but undesirable to high communication apprehensives. Similar variability in degree of area interaction is found in other types of housing too, in apartment complexes, mobile home parks, or housing developments. However, some people select housing areas away from neighbors not because they are high communication apprehensives but simply because they don't desire interaction with neighbors.

In conclusion, from the behaviors of high and low communication apprehensives, we can draw some generalized profiles of each. The high communication apprehensive tends to avoid classes that require a lot of interaction and avoid discussion in small groups; when they do communicate in either situation they may make irrelevant comments; they sit where interaction demands are lowest, select occupations that require little communication with others, date less than others, marry early, and choose housing in a low interaction area. Low communication apprehensives select classes in which interaction will be high, communicate and perhaps dominate in small group discussions, sit where they can control and participate in the communication, select occupations with high communication demands, date often, marry later, and choose housing in a high interaction area.

While these profiles are accurate in general, they do not necessarily apply to any single individual with either high or low communication apprehension. Not every high communication apprehensive will engage in all of the profiled behaviors of a high communication apprehensive, and not every low communication apprehensive will engage in all of the profiled behaviors of a low communication apprehensive. Do not assume, therefore, that simply because a person does not take a public speaking course he/she is a high apprehensive. Only if we observe a person engaging in a large number of the profile behaviors are we justified in inferring their level of communication apprehension.

EFFECTS OF COMMUNICATION APPREHENSION

The primary effects of communication apprehension can be divided into two categories: those that are are experienced internally and those external effects that others can observe. We will review each.

Internal Effects

Communication apprehension is a cognitive response to communication that arouses one internally. McCroskey states that "the only effect of CA that is predicted to be universal across both individuals and types of CA is an internally experienced feeling of discomfort" (1984, p. 33). The lower the level of CA, the less the feeling of discomfort. People with low CA will still have physiological arousal about communicating, but their internal feeling is one of excitement or pleasure, not one of discomfort such as the high CA experiences. The internal feeling the high CA individual experiences is one of discomfort, fright, being unable to cope, being inadequate, and possibly being dumb. Common physiological effects associated with this internal fear might be rapid beating of the heart, queasy stomach, increased perspiration, some shakiness, and dry mouth.

High and low communication apprehensives differ in their behaviors relating to social settings.   James J. Woody, Woody and Associates

External Effects

There are three common behavioral responses to the fear of communicating: communication avoidance, communication withdrawal, and communication disruption. A rare, but worth mentioning, behavioral response is one called overcommunication. Our discussions have touched on all of these, but we will summarize here.

If a person is fearful of someone or something, a very common response is to avoid that person or situation. This is often the case for high CAs. They choose (either intentionally or unintentionally) to avoid communication with others whenever possible. They choose to avoid situations that might require them to communicate. For example, they will avoid classes that have required speeches and teachers who call upon students to answer questions in class. They will avoid occupations that require a high level of communication.

Since avoidance is not always possible, the high CA might withdraw from the communication situation. Often the high CA will find her/himself in a situation that requires communication. Hence they will withdraw by not answering questions or giving minimal communication. This is common in the classroom. The high CA student will avoid communication with her/his teacher when possible. When this is not possible, the student will often not respond to a teacher's question or will give minimal or even wrong responses. This almost always guarantees that the teacher will leave the high CA student alone. However, the teacher generally does not have a positive impression of the high CA student because of this type of withdrawal behavior.

Communication disruption is when the person has disfluencies in verbal speech or unusual nonverbal behaviors. For example, it might seem as if they have a stutter or can't remember what they were going to say or they might get a twitch in their cheek or bite their nails or look anywhere but at the receiver. All of the above could also be responses from a person who has poor communication skills. Hence, this behavior is not as good a predictor of CA as the other two.

Overcommunication is very rare for the high CA individual. However, there are instances in which a person extremely high in CA conceals it by talking all the time. The first two effects discussed here, avoidance and withdrawal, involve the *flight syndrome*. In other words, the high CA decides to avoid or withdraw to take flight from communication. In the overcommunication syndrome the high CA is fighting back by talking all he or she can. They may or may not have a lot to say—they just talk a lot. Usually their communication is ineffective and often they are seen as unskilled communicators.

In conclusion, the CA individual experiences both internal and external effects, both of which are debilitating. We now need to look at the causes of traitlike and state communication apprehension.

CAUSES OF COMMUNICATION APPREHENSION

Now that we have discussed the effects of communication apprehension, we can turn our attention to the causes. We will discuss the causes of traitlike CA and the causes of state/situational CA.

Causes of Traitlike CA

As with shyness, heredity appears to be a meaningful contributor to trait-like CA (McCroskey and Richmond, 1978, 1980, 1982). Children are born with certain personality predispositions, such as sociability. How this sociability is treated by parents can often determine whether a child will develop high CA or not. The predisposition exists, but environment also plays a major role.

How and when the child is reinforced for communication will determine to some extent whether the child will develop high CA or not. If a child is reinforced for communicating, he or she will probably communicate more. However, if the child is punished for communication or the communication is ignored, he or she might communicate less. This simple reinforcement theory alone, however, does not account for CA development.

Many children receive mixed cues or inconsistent punishment and reward for communication. As a result they cannot predict what or when to communicate. They learn to be helpless because of the inconsistent reinforcement patterns of their parents, teachers, peers, and so on. There is no predictability on how or what to communicate, so they avoid communicating with others. For example, little Johnny is allowed to talk during the TV news one night at the dinner table, the next night he is punished for it, two nights later he is allowed to talk again. If this type of inconsistent reinforcement pattern continues in other communication facets of Johnny's life, it is likely he will learn the only way to win is to withdraw. He has learned to be apprehensive about communication.

Causes of Situational Communication Apprehension

The causes of situational or state CA are numerous and can vary from one person to another from one situation to another. We will discuss only the primary causes of situational CA. We will use the major causes of CA as outlined by Buss (1980). They are novelty, formality, subordinate status, conspicuousness, unfamiliarity, dissimilarity, and degree of attention from others.

The novel situation will usually cause an individual some anxiety because he/she does not know how to react or communicate. For example, going for a job interview might be novel for a lot of people, and they will probably be quite nervous. After a person has been to a few job interviews, he/she will be less nervous and know what to predict. It is the uncertainty or unpredictability of the situation that creates the state anxiety.

Formal situations will increase anxiety because there is very little latitude for deviation from the norm. Hence, a person's state CA will increase because he/she does not want to communicate inappropriately. We have all experienced that formal situation in which you know if you communicate inappropriately you will be publicly embarrassed.

Subordinate status is when a person holds "high status" over another. An example of this is when an important public official (the president of the United States) meets with a citizen to discuss issues. The citizen might experience situational shyness. Buss states, "a common outcome is gaze aversion, shrinking from close contact, and an inability to converse normally—in brief, shyness" (p. 188).

Would you like to stand on a crowded street corner naked? The answer is probably no. Almost nothing makes one more nervous and anxious than feeling conspicuous. Being a new person in class makes one conspicuous. Being the person singled out to answer a question in an important meeting makes one conspicuous. As we feel more conspicuous our anxiety level tends to escalate.

Being unfamiliar with the norms in a culture can make one uncomfortable. For example, one of the authors has traveled extensively to other countries and always comments on how uncomfortable he feels when trying to communicate in a different culture because he is not familiar with their norms for communication. If you feel uncomfortable with another anxiety increases. As unfamiliarity increases so does state apprehension.

Dissimilarity is an extension of unfamiliarity. The more dissimilar we are to others, the more difficulty we have communicating with them. As dissimilarity increases so does anxiety.

Most of us like attention from others. However, few of us want to be the center or focus of attention all the time. This makes us very uncomfortable and uneasy. We like a moderate amount of attention. If attention is too high, our anxiety increases.

We have discussed some of the common causes of state communication apprehension. Daly and Hailey (1980) introduced two more. They are degree of evaluation and prior history. For example, if one feels she/he is constantly being evaluated, then her/his communication anxiety will be increased. Also, if one has a prior history of failure with a certain group or individual, the anxiety will be increased when confronting that group or individual.

In conclusion, situational communication apprehension may be caused by a number of elements. However, the elements that cause state CA for one may not cause it for another. We know that in everyday life negative reactions from others, novelty, conspicuousness, and unfamiliar situations can make one anxious about communicating. We have to learn methods of coping with the various communication contexts that make us nervous. Chapter 7 will explore various methods for helping people reduce communication anxiety.

5

Impact of Communication Apprehension and Shyness

In the previous two chapters we have discussed the profiles of high and low communication apprehensives and viewed the behaviors of shy people. However, we have not discussed how these make a difference. This chapter will review the effects of communication apprehension and shyness on interpersonal relations, the everyday environment, and the work environment. While reading this chapter, keep in mind that communication apprehension is a cognitive feeling of anxiety while shyness is the behavior of being quiet or withdrawing from communication situations. In this chapter we will be looking at the impact of both CA and shy behaviors in communication situations.

INTERPERSONAL PERCEPTIONS

Verbal behavior is extremely important in the development of interpersonal relationships and perceptions. As we noted earlier, generally the more a person talks the more positively that person will be perceived, unless the content of what is said is offensive. In the beginning of an interpersonal relationship, sometimes referred to as the "acquaintance stage" of the relationship, the impact of verbal behavior is vital. Since the two people do not know one another, they are uncertain how to react to one another. The primary way this uncertainty can be reduced is to look and listen. If one person chooses not to talk or to talk very little, the other remains uncertain about how to relate to that person. Frequently in such situations the partner of the quiet person simply chooses to terminate the relationship. That is the line of least resistance.

Uncertainty makes most people uncomfortable. We tend to make an effort to resolve the uncertainty. In most instances people must talk to learn more about each other. Those who do not talk enough not only fail to eliminate their own uncertainty, but also may be perceived in a less positive manner by others. High communication apprehensives, because of their tendency to avoid communication, tend to produce negative perceptions in the minds of others. Low communication apprehensives, because of their desire for communication, tend to produce positive perceptions in others. While these differential perceptions may be altered in time, as people get better acquainted, relationships are often terminated due to initial negative perceptions before the time needed to know one another has passed.

So far we have considered perceptions only in general. At this point we will consider specific perceptions and how high and low communication apprehensives are seen to be different by other people. Since the research on communication apprehension and that on shy behavior in general has generated the same results, we will refer in this chapter to high communication apprehensives as quiet people and low communication apprehensives as talkative people. By changing the terminology at this point, we hope to emphasize the fact that it is differences in communication *behavior* that generate differences in perceptions, not just differences in apprehension levels. Whether the differences in communication behavior are produced by communication apprehension or by such things as skill deficiencies, social introversion, cultural divergence, or alienation, the differential communication behaviors will result in differential perception of quiet versus talkative people.

Competence

Quiet people are perceived by others as less competent that talkative people. In the United States culture, and several other cultures where research has been conducted, it has been found that people have a stereotype of quiet people as being less competent and less intelligent than talkative people. It is important that we recognize that this is a stereotype, not a factually based observation. Several researchers have attempted to demonstrate that there is a positive relationship between intelligence and the amount a person talks. No meaningful relationship has been found. Nevertheless, quiet people may be perceived as less competent and less intelligent than their counterparts—the talkative individuals. Such perceptions have been demonstrated in interpersonal and small-group contexts as well as in work and school environments.

Although these perceptions are based on faulty stereotypes, it should be recognized that such perceptions can sometimes lead to self-fulfilling prophecies. In elementary schools, for example, it has been demonstrated that if teachers expect a child to do well, it is increasingly likely the child will do well. The reverse is also true. To some extent, then, we become what others perceive and expect us to be.

Although there is no relationship between talkativeness and competence in general, there is one exception to this rule. That is in the area of communication competence. Talkative people are perceived to be more communicatively competent, and the perception is generally an accurate one. Quiet people accept fewer opportunities to practice their communication skills, and to the extent practice helps improve skill, their communication skills might be less well developed. In contrast, talkative people look for opportunities to practice and refine their communication skills.

Anxiety

Quiet people are perceived to be more anxious about communication than talkative people. Unlike the perceptions concerning intelligence and general competence, these perceptions frequently are accurate. Although not all quiet people are apprehensive about communication, a large proportion are. People generalize this tendency of quiet people to be apprehensive into a stereotype for all quiet people—a stereotype that is shared even by quiet people when reporting their perceptions of other quiet people. Quiet people are also perceived to be less extroverted and less composed. Such perceptions are more likely to be accurate than inaccurate, but this does not mean that they can be generally applied to all quiet people.

Social Style

Social style refers to the way a person is perceived to relate to other people. There are two primary dimensions of social style—assertiveness and responsiveness (see Chapter 6 for more discussion). Assertiveness refers to a person's ability to state opinions with conviction and to be able to defend one's opinions and oneself. Responsiveness refers to a person's willingness to be responsive or open to another during interpersonal interaction.

Quiet people are perceived to be lower in both assertiveness and responsiveness. Talkative people are perceived to be higher in both. These perceptions appear to be accurate. Research indicates that over half of the people identified as low in both assertiveness and responsiveness are high communication apprehensives. In addition, 70 percent of the people identified as high communication apprehensives have been found to be low in both assertiveness and responsiveness. In short, quiet people are accurately perceived as people who have difficulty expressing their opinions to others with conviction and responding to others in an open and sensitive way. Talkative people generally are perceived in an opposite manner.

Leadership

Talkative people are more likely to be perceived as leaders than quiet people. To function as a leader in most situations requires at least a moderate degree of communication with other people. Thus, it is not surprising that people who do not talk much are not perceived to function as leaders. The perception is correct more often than not.

It is interesting to note, however, that in some instances relatively quiet people can function as leaders at least to some degree. For example, the information they provide can change the course of a group discussion and alter the ultimate decision of the group. Even in such an instance, however, the quiet person is not perceived by other group members as the leader. In fact, several research studies have found that other group members may not even remember that the quiet person provided the needed information—they may report that the information came from a more talkative group member. The reason for this conclusion is the talkative person picks up on the idea introduced by the quiet person and runs with it, while the quiet person sits quietly by and watches.

Another type of leadership, opinion leadership, is also important to consider. An opinion leader is someone to whom we turn for information or advice when we need to make a decision. Talkative people are much more likely to be perceived as opinion leaders than quiet people. Again, the perception is probably accurate in more cases than not. Quiet people are unlikely to go out of their way to offer opinions, and since they are perceived by others as less competent, they are less likely to be asked for their opinions concerning an issue or a decision.

Attractiveness

Quiet people are perceived to be less sociable and friendly than are talkative people. As we noted previously, communication is a vital element in reducing uncertainty in human relationships. A reduced level of communication appears to be interpreted by most people as a sign of unfriendliness. Not surprisingly, therefore, quiet people are perceived as less attractive than are talkative people. It is interesting to note this perception is held not only by more talkative people but also by quiet people themselves, who not only see other quiet people as unattractive, but also view themselves as less attractive than more talkative people.

There may be situtations in which a person may choose not to communicate with others.   WVU Photographic Services

From the perceptions we have outlined above, we can draw perceptual profiles of the quiet and talkative person. The quiet person is perceived to be less competent in general, less communicatively competent, more anxious about communication, less composed and extroverted, less assertive and responsive, not either a leader in general or an opinion leader, less sociable and friendly, and less attractive. The talkative person is perceived to be more competent in general, more communicatively competent, less anxious about communication, more composed and extroverted, more assertive and responsive, generally a leader and an opinion leader, more friendly and sociable, and more attractive.

Some of these perceptions are probably accurate in many instances, others are overgeneralized, stereotypical perceptions. Whether right or wrong, however, the perceptions exist and have a direct impact on the everyday lives of talkative and quiet people.

EVERYDAY LIFE

People do not react to us as we are, they react to us as they perceive us to be. We may be more competent than the people around us, but if others perceive us to be less competent, we will be treated as less competent. This is a fact of life in human relationships, whether we like it or not. Relationships are built on perceptions, not reality. Perceptions are based in a large part on communication behavior. We have already noted the common impact on perception of the communication behaviors of quiet and talkative people. At this point we turn to the impact of these perceptions on three important aspects of everyday life—the school environment, the social environment, and the work environment.

School Environment

As we have noted previously, people who are quiet are perceived to be less competent and less intelligent than more talkative people. Such perceptions have a direct impact in the school environment. Although there is at least some positive impact (e.g., quiet children are less likely to get into trouble with the teacher), most of the impact is very negative.

In general, teachers expect quiet children to do less well in school and as a result may treat the quiet child as if he/she were less intelligent. The quiet child is less likely to be called upon to respond in class, thus having less opportunity to correct mistakes in learning. The quiet child receives less attention from the teacher, and thus less reinforcement when he/she does something well. Because of their desire to avoid communication with their teachers, quiet children also ask for assistance less frequently and volunteer to participate less frequently, thus having less opportunity to learn and be reinforced. While this impact is present in education at all levels, it may be most severe in elementary grades. Quiet children often are incorrectly perceived as poor readers or lazy students and thus placed in "slow" groups. Many are never able to overcome this poor start, and they become what they were incorrectly perceived as being—the slow student.

Because many courses are graded at least partially on "participation," quiet people often receive lower grades than their more talkative peers, even though their achievement may actually be equal or even superior to that of their peers. In a very real sense, quiet people are discriminated against in the school environment. The impact of this discrimination is cumulative over the years of schooling. Consequently, by the time young people complete high school, their learning, as measured by standardized achievement tests, is affected. Even though there is no meaningful difference in intelligence, quiet children on average score lower on precollege achievement tests than do their talkative peers. Some recent research has revealed that the quiet college student is substantially below the talkative college student in grade point average at the end of the first year of college. The ultimate effect of quietness, then, is less learning. While quiet children may ultimately achieve less than their aptitudes would justify, talkative children may achieve at a level above what their aptitudes would justify. Because of their willingness to engage in communication with their teachers and their peers, their opportunities for learning and reinforcement are increased. The ultimate effect of talkativeness, then, is increased learning.

Some recent research has also revealed that the quiet child's peers perceive the quiet child as being less approachable or friendly and less intelligent than the talkative child. This perception begins as early as the third grade and remains throughout the high school levels.

Differential attitudes and behaviors related to communication not only affect students, they also affect teachers. Research has indicated quiet teachers are not liked as well by their students as talkative teachers. This has an impact not only on the way teachers are evaluated but also on their effectiveness. Students are less inclined to follow the recommendations of quiet teachers than they are to follow the recommendations of more talkative ones. It appears quiet teachers, particularly those who are high communication apprehensives, are sensitive to the fact students may respond negatively to them. They overwhelmingly choose to teach in the lower elementary grades. They report they are less afraid to communicate with the younger children than they would be to communicate with children in the upper grades or in high school. Whether these teachers are more effective with little children than they would be with older children is not yet known.

We may summarize what we know about the school environment in the following way. The school environment requires effective communication on the part of both students and teachers. Quiet people tend to fare poorly in this environment, while talkative people tend to fare well.

Social Environment

As we have noted previously, people who are quiet are perceived as less friendly and attractive than more talkative people. It is not surprising, therefore, that quiet people tend to have problems in the social environment. We have already noted quiet people have far less dates than talkative people. They also have far fewer people they can call "friends," less than half as many as their more talkative peers.

Social relationships require a certain degree of communication between people to be established and maintained. If someone doesn't want to talk to us, it is natural for us to simply disregard that person and move on to someone else. Visualize, if you can, a very quiet person in a singles' bar or at a cocktail party. How many new people do you think he/she would meet? Now contrast this by visualizing a talkative person in the same setting.

In a study of over 400 college students, quiet and talkative students were asked to indicate how many people they knew whom they would classify as "good friends." Responses ranged from none to over 20. Of particular interest here is the fact that over a third of the high communication apprehensives reported having no good friends at all, while not a single low communication apprehensive reported having no good friends. When asked to list the names of their good friends, over half of those named by the high communication apprehensives were relatives such as parents, siblings, or cousins. Less than 5 percent of the low communication apprehensives mentioned any relatives in this category. They seemingly didn't even bother to count such people.

We may summarize what we know about the social environment in the following way. The social environment requires effective communication for the establishment of good social relationships. Quiet people tend to fare poorly in this environment, talkative people tend to fare well.

Work Environment

As we have noted previously, people who are quiet are perceived to be less competent, less likely to be leaders, less assertive and responsive, and less attractive than more talkative people. The impact of these perceptions may be felt most strongly in the work environment.

Since quiet people tend to choose occupations with low communication requirements and talkative people tend to choose occupations with higher communication requirements, we might assume the impact of their differential communication behaviors would be negated in this environment. Such is not the case.

The nonreticent person is very likely to make a good impresssion in an interview.

James J. Woody, Woody and Assoicates

To begin with, quiet people are less likely to be offered an interview for a position than are talkative people. To be referred to as "quiet" or "reticent" in a recommendation for a job is almost the "kiss of death." With other qualifications being equal, another applicant will be given the interview. In fact, even if other qualifications are not equal, this is likely to be the outcome.

Once an interview is obtained, the road to employment does not become smooth for quiet persons. Their communication behavior in the interview is highly likely to generate negative perceptions of the types we have discussed previously. The talkative person, on the other hand, is very likely to make a good impression in the interview, particularly if he or she does not greatly overdo it.

The above should not be taken to indicate that quiet people do not obtain jobs or that the thousands of people on our unemployment rolls are all quiet people. Usually quiet people do obtain employment. But the positions they obtain typically provide lower status and pay than positions obtained by more talkative people. This is partly a function of the quiet person seeking a position with low communication demands, since such positions generally are lower status, lower pay positions. However, it is also partly a function of employers' unwillingness to hire a quiet person for a better position in the organization.

Once employed, quiet people and talkative people are not equally successful. Research in a wide variety of occupations has indicated quiet people report lower job satisfaction than the average employee, while talkative people report higher than average satisfaction. In many instances, actual job performance quality differs as well. For example, talkative people are far more successful in sales and administrative positions, as would be expected. Quiet people fare somewhat better in routine, nonsupervisory positions. When it comes time for a promotion, the differences between quiet people and talkative people become most dramatic. Research has indicated that not only are quiet people not promoted frequently but also they usually do not anticipate being promoted or even want to be promoted. Most promotions require increased communicative responsibilities involving supervision, and everyone sees the quiet person as a poor candidate for such a position, including the quiet person. Talkative persons, on the other hand, are prime candidates for promotion and tend to populate the upper levels of most organizations.

Finally, it has been found that quiet people tend to retain positions with the same organization for shorter periods than talkative people. In one investigation, for example, after controlling for age, talkative people were found to have 50 percent more seniority than quiet people.

We may summarize what we know about the work environment in the following way. The work environment requires effective communication to obtain and retain employment. Quiet people tend to fall into a "last to be hired, last to be promoted, first to be fired" pattern similar to that of several minority groups against whom systematic discrimination has been practiced. Talkative people find it easier to obtain quality employment, tend to be successful in their work, and are likely to be retained and promoted.

From the effects we have outlined above, we can, once again, draw profiles of the quiet person and the talkative person. The talkative person is successful in the school environment, establishes good social relationships, and is successful in the world of work. The quiet person is less successful in school, has difficulty establishing interpersonal relationships, and has difficulty obtaining and retaining employment.

On the basis of all of this, it would be easy to conclude that the talkative person is always happy, a well-adjusted model to emulate, and the quiet person is a poor, unfortunate soul who is to be pitied. This conclusion, in fact, has been drawn by many. However, it is also challenged by many people, both quiet and talkative. Many quiet people, when offered help to overcome their problem, respond with a firm "No, thank you!" They like themselves just the way they are. They have adjusted their lifestyles to accommodate their quietness and have no interest in changing. Some talkative persons, on the other hand, indicate that their supposedly ideal life is not all ideal. They complain that their propensity to approach all situations with an open mouth often gets them in trouble. Some find themselves in such high-powered, demanding positions that they are soon prime candidates for ulcers, migraine headaches, and heart attacks. Nevertheless, most quiet people consider their quietness a problem, while most talkative people do not consider their talkativeness a problem. This has led communication researchers to attempt to devise ways of helping quiet people become less quiet. Some of these methods are outlined in the last chapter of this text. However, before we look at methods of helping quiet people be less quiet, we need to review how communication apprehension and shyness impact communication effectiveness.

CHAPTER

6

Communication Avoidance and Communication Effectiveness

Most people in modern societies have a strong desire to be competent communicators. While communication scholars are far from being in agreement as to what actually constitutes "communication competence," non-scholars are nearly unanimous in agreeing that to be competent is to be an effective communicator—to accomplish one's purposes through communication.

Exactly what it takes to be an effective communicator has been the subject of countless research efforts and thousands of published articles and books. In fact, the oldest essay ever discovered, written about 3000 B.C., consists of advice on how to speak effectively. This essay was inscribed on a fragment of parchment addressed to Kagemni, the eldest son of the Pharaoh Huni. Similarly, the oldest extant book is a treatise on effective communication. This book, known as the Precepts, was written in Egypt about 2675 B.C. by Ptah-Hotep for the use of the Pharaoh's son. Some of the greatest scholars of antiquity, including Plato, Aristotle, and Cicero, focused much of their attention on what constitutes effective communication. Thus, our understanding of effective communication is drawn from nearly 5000 years of contributions from some of the greatest scholars in human history, and this concern with determining the various aspects of communication effectiveness has continued to the present.

With all of this concern and effort, you might think we would now know exactly what it takes to be an effective communicator in any given situation. Unfortunately, that is not the case. Given the number of possible communicators, topics, and contexts, an almost infinite number of possible communication situations exist. Thus, being able to determine precisely what will make a communicator effective in every possible situation probably is beyond human potential. We can, however, suggest that communication competence is "adequate ability to pass along or give information; the ability to make known by talking or writing" (McCroskey & McCroskey, 1986, p. 1). In addition, there are two ways of determining competence. The first approach asks individuals to self-report their perceptions of their communication competence (self-perceived communication competence). The second approach looks at how individuals perceive that they would behaviorally respond in situations (social style of individuals and immediacy behaviors). Each of these approaches will be reviewed and outcomes discussed. First, however, we can outline some of the elements that appear to be important contributors to effectiveness regardless of the situation.

CONTRIBUTORS TO COMMUNICATION EFFECTIVENESS

Three major elements appear to have the most impact on the development of effective communication. These are behavioral skills, cognitive skills, and orientations toward communication. We will consider each in turn.

Behavioral Skills

Certain communication skills are essential to effective communication. Most of these are obvious and some receive considerable attention in modern educational systems. Such things as acquisition of the language of the culture in which one lives, learning appropriate articulation skills, and overcoming speech problems (voice disorders, stuttering, etc.) are critical. Other skills such as typing, telephone usage, and use of a word processor can also be vitally important, although not as central as the previously mentioned skills for most people.

Skills such as the ones noted above are essentially behavioral in nature. They are the foundation upon which effective communication can be built. Some are formally taught in schools, while others are learned primarily through association with parents and others in one's culture. Although there is much room for improvement in the handling of these skills by our educational systems, a remarkably high percentage of people do develop at least adequate levels of these skills by the time they reach adulthood. Unfortunately, acquisition of these skills is only a step toward becoming an effective communicator, not a guarantee an individual will become one.

Cognitive Skills

Cognitive skills are central to becoming truly effective in communication. Such skills involve understanding the communication process and being able to make appropriate choices of what to communicate and what not to communicate depending on the context and situation. Some of the most basic and important cognitive skills are developing an understanding of how differently words are used by different people, how nonverbal messages are used in one's culture, when it is appropriate and beneficial to assert oneself, and how one may communicate friendliness to another. This list of cognitive skills that can assist one in becoming a more effective communicator is far from complete, of course, but it is illustrative of the types of skills that are important.

As was the case with behavioral skills, cognitive communication skills can be learned through formal instruction in the schools and/or through experience in communication with other people in one's culture. The latter method is essentially trial and error, and it provides no guarantee one will learn the appropriate information. Formal instruction in the cognitive skills related to communication effectiveness is very limited in most of our school systems, including our colleges and universities. Most formal instruction focuses on behavioral skills, and in many schools no formal instruction related to the cognitive aspect of communication is available at all. It should not be surprising, therefore, that the overwhelming majority of people in modern society are not communicatively competent.

Affective Orientations

The final element critical to the development of communication competence is the individual's affective orientations toward communication. By this we mean the person's feelings about and attitudes toward communication.

A person normally has to want to be an effective communicator and care whether he/she is effective in order to actually be effective. All of the behavioral and cognitive skills in the world will not make a person an effective communicator if he or she does not want to be one. There must be a desire in the individual to have an impact on others or the person simply is not likely to be motivated to use whatever behavioral and cognitive skills he or she has. This desire must be coupled with the requisite communication skills, of course—desire alone does not make one an effective communicator.

In Chapter 4 we discussed the other critical affective orientation toward communication: communication apprehension. People who are afraid to communicate are very unlikely to be effective communicators. As we noted, if one is afraid to communicate, no amount of behavioral or cognitive skill will make that person an effective communicator. On the other hand, just because a person is not apprehensive about communication does not mean the person will be an effective communicator. Lower levels of communication apprehension will simply allow the individual to use whatever skills he or she possesses, it will not magically produce new skills. Because communication apprehension serves as such a strong inhibitor of effective communication, many people believe it is the single most significant barrier to effective communication in modern society.

In the following sections we will consider components that we believe are central to effective communication and discuss how communication apprehension tends to reduce the probability an individual will use these. We will focus on the constructs of self-perceived communication competence, social style, and immediacy.

SELF-PERCEIVED COMMUNICATION COMPETENCE

It is often argued that the best way to find out something about someone is to simply ask her or him. This is probably true in the case of communication competence. McCroskey and McCroskey (1986) have developed the Self-Perceived Communication Competence scale (SPCC, see Appendix I). The SPCC is composed of twelve items. The items were chosen to reflect four basic communication contexts—public speaking, talking in a large meeting, talking in a small group, and talking in a dyad—and three common types of receivers—strangers, acquaintances, and friends. For each combination of context and receiver type, people are asked to estimate their communication competence on a 0-100 scale. In addition to a global self-perceived communication competence score, the scale permits generation of a subscore for each type of communication context and receiver.

Studies by McCroskey and his associates have indicated total SPCC scores have been found to correlate significantly positively with self-esteem, willingness to communicate, general attitude toward communication, argumentativeness, and sociability. Similarly, significant negative correlations have been found with communication apprehension, alienation, anomia, neuroticism, introversion, and shyness.

These results suggest a substantial involvement of personality in an individual's perception of her/his communication competence. The strong correlation with willingness to communicate also suggests the potential of the meaningful impact of self-perceived communication competence on actual communication behavior. For example, the higher self-perceived competence one has with strangers the more likely they would be to approach strangers and communicate with them. Similarly, the negative correlation between CA and SPCC suggests that the higher the apprehension the lower the self-perceived communication competence.

It is important to recognize that how competent a person thinks he or she is *not* necessarily related to how competently the person will communicate in any given situation. We have all met buffoons who are very incompetent but think they are very competent. Nevertheless, how competent a person thinks he or she is is very much associated with the person's desire to communicate. Hence, self-perceived competence may in many cases be more important than actual, behavioral competence.

SOCIAL STYLE

The effective interpersonal communicator exhibits three important elements in her/his communication: assertiveness, responsiveness, and versatility. Significant emerging research points to the centrality of these three elements. The most significant research was initiated by Dr. David W. Merrill in 1966 when he was president of Personnel Predictions and Research, Inc. (Personel Predictions and Research, Inc., became part of the The TRACOM Corp. in 1978; Merrill and Reid, 1981; Newton, 1986). This research has produced an immense body of data concerning interpersonal effectiveness under the label of "social style." Others, such as William B. Lashbrook and his colleagues at Wilson Learning Corporation, have also studied social style. Still others have studied similiar concepts under the label of "androgyny" or "psychological gender." Although these bodies of literature have appeared totally independently until very recently, they have measured remarkably similar constructs and drawn conclusions about communication effectiveness that are also very similar. We will consider each of the three central elements below.

Assertiveness

Assertiveness is the capacity to make requests; actively disagree; express positive or negative personal rights and feelings; initiate, maintain, or disengage from conversations; and stand up for one's self without attacking another. In some research this aspect of communication is stereotyped as "masculinity." Of course, such communication behavior is not exclusively performed by males. However, in the American culture the stereotype of appropriate male behavior in communication is closely associated with this characteristic.

A scale related to assertiveness and responsiveness (based on the works of Bem, 1974; Merrill and Reid, 1981; and Wheeless and Dierks-Stewart, 1981) is included in Appendix J. When you examine that measure, note that such things as "defends own beliefs," "acts as a leader," "dominant," and "willing to take a stand" are associated with the assertiveness construct. While such terms do describe the stereotyped male image in American society, they more importantly describe a person who is in control of her/himself and her/his communication.

It is important to distinguish between assertiveness and aggressiveness, since many people confuse the two. Those who communicate assertively stand up for their own rights and present themselves and their ideas forthrightly and strongly. Those who communicate aggressively also do this; however, an aggressive communicator also demands that others yield their rights. A person communicating assertively makes requests. A person communicating aggressively makes demands. A person communicating assertively insists that her/his rights be respected. A person communicating aggressively does the same while ignoring the rights of others.

Research has indicated that both assertiveness and aggressiveness have a strong negative correlation with communication apprehension. That is, the more apprehensive a person is about communication, the less likely he/she is to behave in either an assertive or an aggressive manner. This fact has both good and bad implications for the effectiveness of the high communication apprehensive's communication. Since aggressive communication is very likely to alienate other people, at least the highly apprehensive person is unlikely to face this outcome. On the other hand, unassertive people tend to be taken advantage of or ignored by others, no matter how right they may be. In addition, they tend to be looked upon as ineffectual people by others in their environment.

Engaging in assertive communication behavior prompts other people in an interaction to communicate more, in most cases. Highly apprehensive people, of course, tend to desire to avoid communication, particularly communication that involves interpersonal conflict, since this is what makes them most uncomfortable. Thus, high communication apprehensives often will simply yield their rights (be unassertive) rather than defend them (be assertive) in order to avoid more communication. Consequently, high communication apprehensives frequently are not effective communicators.

Responsiveness

Responsiveness is the capacity to be sensitive to the communication of others, to be seen as a good listener, to make others comfortable in com-

Responsiveness is the capacity to be sensitive to the communication of others, to be seen as a good listener and to recognize the communication needs and desires of others.   WVU Photographic Services

municating, and to recognize the needs and desires of others. In some research this aspect of communication is stereotyped as "femininity." Of course, this does not mean that only females are responsive. However, the communication behaviors most closely associated with responsiveness are very similar to the traditional American stereotype of appropriate communication behaviors for females.

When you examine the measure in Appendix J, note that such qualities as "sympathetic," "compassionate," "gentle," and "friendly" are associated with the responsiveness construct. While such terms do describe the stereotypical female image in American society, they more importantly describe a person who is open to the communication of others and empathic with those others.

It is important we distinguish between responsiveness and submissiveness, since many people confuse the two. Submissiveness is the yielding of one's legitimate rights to another without necessarily receiving anything in return. Responsiveness is recognizing the needs and rights of another without yielding one's own rights. The responsive individual communicates understanding and acknowledgment of the feelings of the other person. The submissive individual may do this also but then go on to yield to the requests of the other person even when it requires that he/she must go against his/her own feelings, rights, or needs.

Considerable research indicates that communication apprehension is correlated with both responsiveness and submissiveness. However, the directions of the correlations are different. Communication apprehension is positively correlated with submissiveness but negatively correlated with responsiveness. The highly communication apprehensive individual is likely to submit to the desires of another because the failure to do so may prompt more communication attempts from the other person, at best, and communication involving conflict, at worst. In order to avoid these outcomes, the highly communication apprehensive individual may simply submit.

In contrast, the highly communication apprehensive individual is much less likely to communicate in a responsive manner. Most of the behaviors that indicate responsiveness are invitations to additional communication, which the person wants to avoid. The primary way in which we communicate responsiveness to others is through immediacy with them, and research has indicated there is a substantial negative correlation between communication apprehension and immediacy in communication. (We will consider immediacy in a later section.) The higher the level of communication apprehension, the less immediacy in the communication of the individual. Consequently, highly communication apprehensive individuals frequently are ineffective communicators. Unfortunately, people who are not immediate and responsive tend to be perceived negatively by others. They typically are seen as cold and unfriendly, even uncaring; consequently, they may not seem attractive as potential friends.

Versatility

The final important characteristic of the effective communicator is versatility. Versatility is the capacity to be *appropriately* assertive and *appropriately* responsive, depending on the situation. People who are versatile in their communication behaviors may be described as accommodating, adaptable, informal, and willing to adjust to others. People not exhibiting versatility in their communication may be described as rigid, inflexible, unyielding, and uncompromising.

Some situations call for high assertiveness, some for high responsiveness. Some situations call for low assertiveness, some for low responsiveness. Some situations call for both high assertiveness and responsiveness, but very few call for low levels of both. Individuals who are versatile in their communication behaviors are able to adapt to these disparate demands of situations. Individuals tend to have habitual communication behavior patterns are insensitive to the varying demands of situations.

Communicating effectively with different people on different topics and at different times requires different communication behaviors. Consider, for example, the situation in which you might be communicating with a highly aggressive individual. Should you be highly assertive in response? Should you be highly responsive? The former choice might lead to confrontation and conflict, the latter to submission. Neither would normally be seen as the "best" way to communicate. The most effective communicator would be assertive when necessary to defend her/his own rights but remain responsive to the other's communication without submitting to unreasonable requests or demands. An outside observer would see the competent individual behaving differently at different points in the interaction.

In contrast to the versatile communicator in the example above, the people lacking versatility in their communication behavior tend to be assertive or nonassertive and responsive or nonresponsive nearly all of the time. Such people may be typed by their characteristic communication behaviors. The person who is characteristically highly assertive but nonresponsive has been labeled "masculine," in keeping with the male stereotype in the American culture. The opposite type, highly responsive but nonassertive, has been labeled "feminine," again in keeping with the female stereotype in the American culture. The "masculine" type usually is thought of as aggressive, while the "feminine" type usually is thought of as submissive.

The person who is characteristically both highly assertive and highly responsive has been labeled "androgynous." While this person is just as strongly typed as the others, in the American culture this type of characteristic communication pattern tends to be much more effective in most cases. This probably is a result of the two sets of behaviors (assertive and responsive) tending to prevent excesses that may come from either. High assertiveness is prevented from becoming aggressiveness by the presence of high responsiveness. Similarly, high responsiveness is prevented from becoming submissiveness by the presence of high assertiveness. While this person may not truly be versatile, as we have described this characteristic above, it is likely he/she will be perceived as such in many cases by others.

At the other end of the continuum is the individual who characteristically is both nonassertive and nonresponsive. This individual also lacks versatility, and unlike the androgynous individual, it is highly unlikely others will see this person as versatile. Research has found a very high proportion of these individuals to be high communication apprehensives (Lashbrook, Knutson, Parsley, and Wenburg, 1976). These individuals are the ones least likely to be effective communicators. The only way these individuals may become more effective communicators is to reduce their communication apprehension.

IMMEDIACY

Immediacy is the degree of perceived physical or psychological closeness between two people. The concept may be best understood in terms of the "immediacy principle" as outlined by Mehrabian (1971), the person who introduced this concept into the literature. This principle is:

> People are drawn toward persons and things they like, evaluate highly, and prefer; and they avoid or move away from things they dislike, evaluate negatively, or do not prefer (p. 1).

In connection with our discussion above, responsive communication behaviors are those that are immediate, and nonresponsive communication behaviors are those that are nonimmediate. Responsiveness on the part of another, then, makes us feel that they like us, evaluate us highly, and prefer to interact with us. In contrast, nonresponsiveness on the part of another makes us feel they dislike us, evaluate us negatively, and prefer not to interact with us. Immediacy behaviors are central to the generation of such perceptions.

Immediacy behaviors, then, are important in two ways. They are the primary means of expressing approval of another, and they provide an invitation to another to continue communication. In order to understand immediacy and its relationship to communication apprehension, avoidance, and effectiveness, it is important we look at specific behaviors that express varying degrees of immediacy.

Verbal Immediacy

What people say can cause us to feel either closer to or more distant from them. Increased immediacy is produced by verbal messages indicating openness to the other, friendship for the other, or empathy with the other. Such simple things as the use of the pronoun "we" rather than "you" or "you and I" can increase feelings of immediacy.

One of the most important ways of increasing immediacy in a relationship is sending verbal messages that encourage the other person to communicate. Such comments as "I see what you mean," "Tell me more," "That is a good point," and "I think so too" will create increased immediacy. Contrast these comments with the following: "Oh, shut up"; "That is stupid"; "I thought of that years ago"; "Frankly, I don't care what you think." If you were to hear any of the latter comments, would you want to communicate more? How close would you feel to the person who made such a comment?

Clearly, the most direct way to modify feelings of immediacy is through verbal messages. However, many nonverbal messages can accomplish the same end, although they often are much less direct. While immediacy is communicated both verbally and nonverbally, the nonverbal component appears to be far more important in most cases. This is because, while the nonverbal may exist independent of any verbal message, verbal messages are almost always accompanied by a variety of nonverbal messages (Richmond, McCroskey, and Payne, 1987). Further, if a verbal message indicates immediacy while nonverbal messages are contradictory, receivers tend to disregard the verbal message. We will consider some of the important nonverbal message systems below.

Nonverbal Immediacy

Space. The amount of physical distance between people is one of the strongest indicators of immediacy. How do you feel when you try to stand or sit close to someone and they keep moving away? Regardless of reason for moving, you probably interpret the behavior as rejection. In order to be perceived as immediate, a person needs to reduce the physical distance between her/himself and the other person. Extremely close physical proximity, of course, is reserved for very intimate communication. To try to establish such extreme closeness in a nonintimate relationship is very likely to be perceived negatively by the other person.

Touch. Touch is the ultimate in reduced physical distance. As such it is the most immediate nonverbal behavior. Many people consider touch to be the most potent form of communication. As a result, when it is appropriate, it strongly communicates immediacy. However, when it is inappropriate, it is very likely to be interpreted negatively. Contrast, for example, a pat on a friend's back for a job well done with a pat on the backside of a stranger in an elevator. Both are touch. One is an appropriate immediacy behavior. The other may prompt a call for the police.

Eye Behavior. Eye contact reduces perceived physical distance. When people look at us when we are talking, we feel closer to them. If their eyes are wandering around the room, we quickly realize they do not care about what we are saying, and possibly not even about us. People sitting eight feet apart with constant eye contact may actually feel closer to one another than people sitting three feet apart with no eye contact. As with space and touch, too much of a good thing may cause problems. Constant eye contact, particularly at close distances, may be interpreted as staring and may make the recipient of the eye contact very uncomfortable.

Facial Expression. In addition to our eyes, the rest of our face can also communicate immediacy. In particular, a smile is seen as a very immediate nonverbal message. A frown, of course, is extremely nonimmediate. We also communicate attention, or lack of same, by our facial expression and eye behavior. This is not just a matter of eye contact, but also the expression around our eyes and mouths. An attentive expression is a strong immediacy behavior.

Gestures and Bodily Movements. The position of your body when communicating with another, your posture, the type and amount of gestures you employ all involve immediacy messages. The person who seems relaxed, has an open body position, uses forward leans when communicating, and gestures in a positive manner is very likely to be perceived as immediate. Nonimmediate behaviors include such things as a closed body position (like arms folded across each other), very little gesturing, and a tense posture. Of course, gestures and bodily movements can be overdone, like most other immediacy behaviors. When they are we sometimes refer to the person as "coming on like gang busters." Such behaviors can become too much and cease being immediate.

Voice. One of the subtlest ways we communicate immediacy is through our voices. A high degree of voice variety is very immediate, while a monotone voice is one of the most nonimmediate communication behaviors. In a recent study we found that the number one nonverbal behavior that distinguished students' perceptions between good and poor teachers was vocal variety. This is also strongly correlated with the amount students reported learning in classes. If people have little vocal animation when they talk with us, they communicate that they do not care about us and/or what they are talking about. We may in turn conclude that we have little reason to care about what they are saying.

Scent. It is clear from the research that odor can evoke emotional and even physical responses from people and animals. Humans have learned to manipulate scent to produce certain reactions. Men and women wear scents they think will attract one another. Researchers generally agree that overpowering scents, offensive scents, and unfamiliar scents tend to make people nonimmediate with others or the environment. We are not as likely

Nonverbal behaviors such as eye contact and smiling communicate immediacy to others.   WVU Photographic Services

to seek immediacy with a person who has offensive body odor or over-powering cologne—we like familiar, subtle scents.

Time. An often overlooked immediacy behavior is the amount of time we spend with someone. For the most part, the more time we spend with another individual, the more immediate we are with them. Contrast, for example, the teacher who is willing to take an extra half-hour in her/his office to explain something to you with the teacher who tells you to look it up in your textbook. You are probably going to see the former teacher as much more immediate.

The relationships between immediacy behaviors and communication apprehension and avoidance are very strong. Since people who are very apprehensive about communicating generally wish to avoid communicating and immediacy behaviors are an invitation to continued communication, such people tend to be much less immediate than others. By being nonimmediate with others in the environment, highly apprehensive individuals cause the others to have a reduced desire to communicate with them—they are seen as unattractive communication targets. Thus, the apprehensive individual is involved in less total communication both because he/she chooses not to initiate communication with others and because the others choose not to initiate communication with him/her.

The reduced immediacy behaviors of highly communication apprehensive people also lead them to be less effective communicators when they do communicate. This may be explained in part by the "principle of reciprocity." In communication situations there is a strong tendency for people to imitate the behavior of others with whom they communicate. In other words, communication patterns tend to be reciprocal—I do what you do and you do what I do. If one person smiles, or exhibits some other immediate behavior, it is increasingly likely the other person will engage in similar behavior. It is often said the best way to make a friend is to be a friend. This is the reciprocity principle in action.

Highly apprehensive individuals have great difficulty engaging in immediate behavior, hence do not communicate positive affect to other people with whom they communicate. Since they are not perceived as liking the other person, there is a tendency for the other person to reciprocate by not liking them very much either. This tends to interfere with the attempts of the apprehensive individual to communicate effectively with the other person at such times as they do try to do so. Quite simply, then, high communication apprehension tends to lead to ineffective communication. The only solution to this problem is to reduce that apprehension. The next chapter is directed toward methods that have been found helpful in accomplishing that objective.

7

Reducing Communication Apprehension

In the preceding chapters of this book, we have discussed the nature of human communication, the impact of avoiding communication, and the relationship of apprehension about communication to both communication avoidance and communication effectiveness. We have noted that for many people communication apprehension is the single most important factor contributing to a lack of effectiveness in communication. In this chapter we will direct our attention to three methods that have been developed to help people reduce their apprehension about communication.

In order to understand the differences in the methods that are used to help people overcome apprehension about communication, we need first to outline briefly the divergent theories concerning why people are apprehensive in the first place. Each of the methods is keyed to a different view of the cause of the problem.

THEORIES OF CAUSES

The basic theories about why people experience fear or anxiety about communication may be placed into three categories: (1) excessive activation, (2) inappropriate cognitive processing, and (3) inadequate communication skills. We will consider each of these in turn.

Excessive Activation

If you can recall the first time you ever had to speak, sing, play a ball game, or otherwise perform before a group of people, you will probably remember your heart beating rapidly, your palms getting wet with sweat, and possibly a slight feeling of queasiness in your stomach. All of these physiological reactions are symptoms of your body becoming activated in preparation for the upcoming performance. Athletes often refer to this as "getting psyched up" before a game. This increase in the physiological activation in your body is altogether normal. In fact, such an increase in activation often is essential to a high quality performance.

However, increased activation is one thing and excessive activation is quite another. Excessive activation occurs when the normal increase in activation in anticipation of a performance continues to a point beyond an individual's ability to control it. In extreme cases people have been known to regurgitate their most recent meal or faint from this excessive activation. In rare instances such excessive activation can even prompt a coronary arrest, better known as a heart attack. Much more commonly, however, excessive activation brings on trembling in the arms, hands, and legs; shortness of breath; dryness in the mouth; difficulty in swallowing; tenseness of muscles; and temporary loss of memory.

From the first theoretical viewpoint, then, these bodily disturbances are what apprehension is—a physiological over-reaction to an upcoming performance. This may be thought of as a purely behavioral interpretation of the problem. There is no mentalistic explanation. What one thinks is of no importance; what one's body is doing is critical.

Since the physiological arousal is the cause of the problem, the obvious solution is to reduce that arousal. Many methods of reducing arousal have been found to be temporarily effective. These include such things hypnotism, meditation, the use of biofeedback, and ingestion of certain drugs. However, learning deep muscular relaxation techniques is seen as having the most long-term positive impact. Such relaxation is a foundational component of a method of treating communication apprehension (and other neurotic and phobic anxieties). This method is known as "systematic desensitization." If one is to operate on the basis of the "excessive activation" theory, this method is very appropriate.

Inappropriate Cognitive Processing

Research has indicated that many people who are highly aroused physiologically do not report being apprehensive about the upcoming communication situation (or other performance) while others with similar high arousal report extreme apprehension. In addition, some people with much lower levels of arousal report high levels of apprehension while others similarly aroused do not.

This has led many people to believe the problem is caused not by one's body, but by one's mind. This view sees people who report experiencing high apprehension in a communication situation as being no different from other people, except that they think they are. In short, this view sees the person who reports experiencing high apprehension as simply processing the available information inappropriately. One person perceives physiological activation as evidence he/she is excited, while another person perceives it as evidence he/she is terrified. The problem, therefore, is in the cognitive processing of the individual.

This theoretical view, then, is a cognitive rather than a behavioral one. The problem is seen as being all in one's mind. Hence, in order to solve the problem, what is needed is to change the person's mind. A method known as "cognitive restructuring," based on this view, has been developed to overcome communication apprehension as well as other neurotic and phobic anxieties.

At first examination it might appear the excessive activation and inappropriate cognitive processing theories are directly contradictory; if one is correct, the other is incorrect. In fact, some people who are strongly committed to one or the other of the theories have argued this position. However, research suggests both are at least partially correct.

An important study by Behnke and Beatty (1981) has shed the most light in this area. In that study the researchers asked subjects who had just given a public speech to indicate how much anxiety they had felt during the speech. The researchers also measured the speakers' levels of physiological activation during the speech (their heart rate) and, as a measure of how they cognitively process information about communication, obtained responses from the subjects on the PRCA.

Research results indicated that heart rates while speaking were not correlated with PRCA scores, suggesting that physiological activation and cognitive processing may not be meaningfully related. Both heart rate and PRCA scores, however, were highly related to the amount of anxiety the subjects reported experiencing while speaking. In fact, the two variables together accounted for almost 80 percent of the variability in self-reported anxiety while speaking.

On the basis of this study, then, it appears these two theories are not in conflict with each other. Rather, it appears both are correct, but may apply differently to different people. Some people experience anxiety while communicating because their bodies are excessively activated. Others experience anxiety because they are cognitively predisposed to interpret whatever activation is present, even if it is low, as indicating they are anxious.

Inadequate Communication Skills

Probably the oldest and most persistent view of why people are apprehensive about communication is that they are fearful and anxious because they do not know how to communicate effectively. There certainly are many people who are deficient in communication skills, particularly the kinds of cognitive communication skills we discussed in Chapter 6. There are also some who are deficient in behavioral skills. If one does not know how to do something but is forced to do it anyway, to be fearful or anxious is a normal reaction. For example, if you do not know how to drive a car but must do so in an emergency, if you are not scared, you are not normal.

The obvious method of helping a person to overcome communication apprehension if it stems from a lack of communication skills is to provide training to improve the skills. That indeed is the method advocated by people who subscribe to this theory.

The major problem with this approach is that research has not provided much evidence in its support. In fact, studies that have involved direct observation of the communication behaviors of high and low apprehensives normally have failed to find any differences in the actual communication skills of the two groups. The subjects in the two groups, however, consistently believe their skill levels are different. The highly apprehensive subjects think their skills are deficient while the subjects with lower apprehension do not. On the basis of direct observation, some in both groups have been found to have high skills, some to have low skills.

Results of research of the type referred to above suggest deficient skills alone may be insufficient to cause apprehension. Thus, it may be that how one thinks about her/his skills is much more important than her/his actual skill level. This, of course, relates back to the inappropriate cognitive processing explanation. This may explain why the skills-training approach that seems to be most effective in helping people is the method known as "rhetoritherapy," developed by Phillips (1977). This method, unlike many other skills approaches, includes a strong component of cognitive restructuring in addition to training involving specific skills.

TREATMENT APPROACHES

A number of books and hundreds of popular press articles have appeared over the past few years professing to help people overcome their shyness, reticence, or communication apprehension. All provide so-called self-help methods that allegedly will allow the reader to solve her/his problem. All evidence indicates that such writings do not work and that in all likelihood one cannot meaningfully and permanently reduce one's communication apprehension without the aid of a professional helper. A careful examination of the research literature fails to produce a single study providing reliable data to the contrary. Real help must come from a formal treatment program under the guidance of a trained professional.

When one thinks of "treatment," it is normal to think of medical treatment. Much medical treatment is based on a physician determining what is wrong with a person and then doing something to the person to overcome the problem such as prescribing a drug or performing an operation. Treatment of communication apprehension is not analogous to medical treatment. The approaches for helping a person reduce his/her level of communication apprehension do not involve "doing something to" the person. Rather, all involve the person in charge of the treatment working with the client in a joint effort to overcome the problem. In this sense, treatment for communication apprehension more closely resembles preventive medicine than medical treatment.

To improve one's health, for example, a physician may outline a diet the person should follow. However, it is up to the individual to follow or not follow the diet. Similarly, in treatment of communication apprehension the person guiding the treatment can outline the steps an individual should follow to obtain improvement, but it is up to the individual to do what is necessary to obtain the desired benefits. In both cases (preventive medicine and treatment for communication apprehension), the individual must want to obtain the benefits and be committed to following the advice of the professional helper for any improvement to occur. In the absence of such commitment, no improvement is likely.

The three most commonly employed methods for treating communication apprehension are (1) systematic desensitization, (2) cognitive restructuring, and (3) skills training. We will explain each of these in turn.

Systematic Desensitization

Systematic desensitization is a behavior therapy originally developed by Wolpe (1958). The method was used in a major study involving apprehension about public speaking by Paul (1966) and introduced as a method of treating more broadly based communication apprehension by McCroskey, Ralph, and Barrick (1970) and McCroskey (1972). It is now the most widely used method in the communication field (Hoffman and Sprague, 1982).

There are two primary components in the systematic desensitization method. The first involves teaching the subjects the procedures for deep muscular relaxation. The second involves having the subjects visualize participating in a series of communication situations while in a state of deep

Almost all of us experience communication apprehension at some time or another.
Greg Ellis, WVU Photographic Services

relaxation. The series of situations is ordered from the least anxiety provoking to the most anxiety provoking. The treatment may be administered either on an individual basis or in a small group, normally 5–7 people. A typical program includes 5 to 7 one-hour sessions spread over several days or several weeks.

In the first session the helper explains the program to the subjects, usually stressing that the treatment does not involve the subject having to engage in any type of communication activity. Rather, it is explained, the subject will learn how to achieve deep muscular relaxation and then will be trained to maintain relaxation while visualizing participating in increasingly more stressful communication experiences. If the subjects have any questions, they are answered and then the actual treatment begins.

Subjects are seated in comfortable chairs and told to lean back and relax. The communication system between the subjects and the helper is then explained. The subjects are told that anytime they feel any tension, once the relaxation instructions have been provided, they are to indicate that to the helper simply by raising the index finger of their right hand. This is also noted as the method of responding to any questions that the helper might ask later in the session.

Once the helper is certain the subjects understand the procedure for communication of tension, he/she turns on a prerecorded tape that includes instructions for deep muscular relaxation. This tape instructs the subjects in how to tense and relax each of the major muscle groups in the body. The total time for this instructional process is about 25 minutes.

When the instructions for relaxation have been completed, the helper turns off the recorder and checks to make certain all of the subjects are awake. This is necessary because in a state of deep relaxation people tend to fall asleep. When the helper is confident all of the subjects are awake and deeply relaxed, he/she reminds them that if at any time they feel any tension they should indicate that to the helper by raising their finger. Then the helper asks the subjects to visualize themselves in the first, least threatening communication situation (something like "You are talking to your best friend"). The helper then remains silent for a period of approximately 15 seconds while watching for finger indications of tension. If any subject signals tension, the helper asks all subjects to put the situation out of their minds and then provides a few moments of relaxation instructions similar to those on the prerecorded tape. If no subject indicates tension for 15 seconds, the helper directs all subjects to put the situation out of their minds and provides a few moments of relaxation instructions before visualizing the situation again.

If any subject signals tension the process of visualization is continuously repeated, as above, until no subject does so for 15 seconds. Then, after a few moments of relaxation instructions, the visualization is repeated with the helper waiting 30 seconds before terminating the visualization unless a subject signals that he/she is experiencing tension. If there is such a signal, the same procedure used with the 15-second interval is employed. The process in repeated until all subjects have been able to visualize the situation for 15 and 30 seconds sequentially without experiencing tension. At this point the helper moves on to the second communication situation and repeats exactly the procedure used with the first one. This process is continued until all of the communication situations have been successfully visualized without tension by all subjects in the group or until the time to end the session is near.

If the number of situations to which the subjects are to be exposed is typical (16–18), the entire list will not be completed in the first session, nor likely even in the first four or five sessions. To complete a given session, the helper will have the subjects visualize a situation they have already successfully visualized without tension for approximately 60 seconds. This will help ensure that the subjects are still deeply relaxed as the session ends. At this point the helper typically asks the subjects to open their eyes and gradually become reacquainted with their surroundings. After the subjects have become more alert, the helper suggests they practice the relaxation exercises daily in between sessions and to try to use them to become relaxed if they confront stressful communication situations during the intervening time period.

In subsequent sessions, the same procedures are followed as in the first session with only minor variation. In later sessions it may not be necessary to play the entire tape of relaxation instructions. This is particularly true if the subjects have been given copies of the tape with which to practice between sessions. Also in later sessions the helper may begin with somewhat more stressful communication situations than the first one. However, any situation that prompted tension in the preceding session should be avoided as a starter in the next session. After two or three sessions helpers often ask the subjects to relate their experiences in attempting to use the techniques they have learned in the sessions in real communication situations. This helps to reinforce in the subjects' minds that they should be making such attempts.

Ideally, sessions should continue until all subjects are able to visualize all of the communication situations without experiencing any tension. If this is accomplished before the scheduled number of sessions (normally 5–7 sessions) has been held, the program can be terminated early. If this has not been accomplished when the last scheduled session has been completed, an additional session or sessions should be added. If one individual in a group seems to be reacting with significantly more tension than the other members, it may be necessary to remove that person from later sessions in order that the remaining group members can complete the entire program. It is relatively rare that such a person is found in a group since the treatment is so highly effective. However, some people are not helped by the method, and a small percentage of these continue to respond with very high tension during the treatment sessions. For these few people, one of the other methods described below should be substituted.

Systematic desensitization is an extremely effective method for helping people overcome communication apprehension. Research indicates approximately 90 percent of the people who receive this treatment reduce their levels of communication apprehension and, of those who enter the treatment as high communication apprehensives, 80 percent are no longer high apprehensives after treatment.

As we noted earlier, systematic desensitization is the most appropriate method of treating communication apprehension if one presumes the problem stems from excessive physiological activation. McCroskey, Ralph, and Barrick (1968) tested to determine the effects of this method on such activation. They found that activation (in this case heart rate) in subjects reporting high anxiety greatly increased as they were exposed to a formal communication situation prior to treatment. However, after treatment these same subjects were able to control their activation so that no similar increase occurred.

The effectiveness of systematic desensitization is not restricted to simply increasing control of activation, however. A number of studies (i.e., McCroskey, 1972) have found cognitive effects in terms of substantially reduced scores on the PRCA. In addition, Goss, Thompson, and Olds (1978) have reported meaningful improvements in communication behavior as well. The exact reason *why* systematic desensitization works remains a subject of scholarly dispute. However, that it *works* and *works well* is clearly established.

Cognitive Restructuring

The method of cognitive restructuring (Meichenbaum, 1976) evolved from an earlier method known as rational-emotive therapy (Ellis, 1962). Both are based upon the idea that people have irrational thoughts about themselves and their behaviors and that these thoughts increase the anxiety a person is likely to have about something such as communicating with others. In rational-emotive therapy the person receiving treatment is encouraged to identify irrational beliefs he/she has about communication, and then these beliefs are attacked logically in an attempt to demonstrate to the individual that he/she should change her/his way of thinking. The assumption is that if the irrational thoughts are eliminated, the apprehension will be reduced. Several research studies indicate that this approach has some positive effect.

The cognitive restructuring approach goes an important step further. In addition to identifying the illogical beliefs held by the individual, the helper assists the individual in formulating new, more appropriate beliefs. This method recognizes that simple elimination of illogical beliefs may not be enough and that the replacement of displaced beliefs by more appropriate beliefs is an important positive step.

Like systematic desensitization, cognitive restructuring typically is administered in 5 or 6 one-hour sessions spread over several days or weeks. Treatment may be administered to people on an individual basis or in small groups, typically 4–8 people. As outlined by Fremouw (1984), the treatment involves four steps: introduction of the person being treated to the method, identification of negative self-statements (illogical beliefs), learning coping statements (beliefs to replace the illogical ones), and practice.

During the first session the helper gives the subjects in the treatment a thorough rationale and purpose for the program. He/she explains that communication apprehension is a learned reaction that most people can change in a few hours. It is explained that people mentally talk to themselves and that the self-statements they make may be completely irrational and harmful. Finally, it is explained that by learning positive coping statements to substitute for the harmful ones, the subjects can reduce their apprehension.

Following this introduction, the subjects are led to identify specific negative self-statements or thoughts that may increase one's apprehension. The helper provides a large number of examples to illustrate the kind of statement under consideration; for instance, "I'll die if I have to give a speech"; "This interview is the most important thing in my life"; "No one will like me if I don't do well"; "I don't know how to ask for a date." After the subjects understand what negative self-statements are, they are each asked to identify and write down three or four that they commonly make to themselves. These are then discussed by the helper in terms of how they might affect a person's feeling about communication as well as his/her behavior. Logical errors ("If everyone does not agree with me, I have failed") and self-fulfilling prophecies ("I will do a miserable job") are pointed out also. At the conclusion of the first session, the subjects are asked to try to remember the negative self-statements they make to themselves regarding communication between then and the next session. They are encouraged to write down such statements and bring them to the next session.

The second session begins with a discussion of the negative self-statements that the subjects bring in as examples of statements they have used since the previous session. This is handled in much the same way as were the negative self-statements in the first session. When this is completed, the helper works with the subjects to generate positive self-statements (coping statements) which can be substituted for the negative ones. Different groups of statements are generated for use before the communication event, during it, and after it is over. Examples of such statements might be: "Most of these people really want to hear my ideas. This really is quite easy. I did a good job." At the conclusion of this session, the subjects are encouraged to attempt to substitute the positive self-statements for negative ones when communicating with others before the next session.

The remaining sessions are devoted to guided practice in using the coping statements. Subjects are placed in groups (unless they are already in a group for treatment) and asked to discuss topics of an increasingly controversial nature. The subjects are also asked to keep a diary identifying stressful communication situations they have experienced both within the treatment sessions and between sessions and the coping statements they have used in those situations. When all of the subjects report they have been able to use coping statements in stressful communication situations, the practice sessions are terminated and the treatment program is complete.

Research involving cognitive restructuring indicates it is effective in accomplishing its specific objective, reducing self-reported apprehension about communication. Its effectiveness seems to be roughly equal to that of systematic desensitization in this regard. There is evidence cognitive restructuring also reduces observable manifestations of anxiety in actual communication encounters. Some treatment programs have been developed that include both of these methods. Research indicates that the two together are more effective with more people than is either alone, but there is as yet insufficient data to be certain this is the case.

Skills Training

Unlike the two previously outlined treatment methods, which have generally accepted, formalized procedures, there are so many approaches to skills training it is difficult to outline what this method specifically includes or excludes. Programs labeled as "skills training" vary from a whole college course on communication skills to a few hours of training in order to call a person to ask for a date. Before we attempt to outline characteristics that a typical skills training program might include, we need to turn our attention to the effectiveness of this approach generally.

The oldest and most widely used version of this treatment method is courses in speech or communication skills provided by high schools and colleges. In many instances these courses are required of all students in the school or in a given major. Survey research conducted with American adults suggest this form of skills training is almost wholly ineffective in reducing communication apprehension. In fact, our respondents regularly indicate that the course either had no effect on their level of apprehension about communication or made it worse.

In contrast, numerous studies involving skills training for such specific things as increasing assertiveness and learning to ask for a date have brought about major improvement in communication behavior and at least a modest reduction in apprehension about the specific type of communication addressed in the treatment. Notably, in almost all of this research the subjects have volunteered for treatment and were not required to participate. They had been self-identified as skill deficient in the treatment area.

We believe the differences in the effects of these two divergent types of skills training stem from two factors. The first is the need for willing cooperation of the person being treated. The second relates to the need for skills training to have narrowly defined targets for improvement.

As we noted previously, for any treatment program to be successful, the recipient of the treatment must want to improve and be committed to following the advice of the professional helper. In the studies where skills training has been found to be most effective, the volunteer subjects had such a commitment. In contrast, data from our surveys of American adults indicate that most of them only took the speech or communication skills courses because they were required to do so. The people who found the courses beneficial were primarily those who reported not having a high level of communication apprehension to begin with. Of the relatively small number who said they did have a high level of communication apprehension and a course helped reduce it, virtually all had voluntarily taken the course rather than taking it as a requirement. These data suggest, therefore, that the skills training programs that involve whole skills courses are not necessarily ineffective. Their lack of success may be with the students who are in the program either not needing it or not wanting it.

The other factor distinguishing the two broad types of skills training programs relates to the definition of the target for improvement. Research in this area indicates the more narrowly the target behavior is defined, the greater the probability improvement will occur. In many skills-based courses the behaviors to be improved are very poorly defined. "To present an effective speech" or "To conduct an employment interview" are not unusual statements of objectives in such courses. These are much too broad to be specific training targets. While these may be general goals of such courses, for skills training to be effective these broad behavioral goals must be broken down to specific behaviors that can be identified and learned.

Before we look at skills training as an approach helping people to reduce communication apprehension, we need to make completely clear the *primary* purpose of skills training. It is to improve skills. Thus, a skills training program that can be demonstrated to improve skills should be judged successful, even if no impact on communication apprehension occurs at all. In some studies, this is the type of result that has been obtained. In others, some reduction in communication apprehension has also been observed.

Because skills training is time consuming for both the professional helper and the person being treated, and thus tends to be expensive, its use as a method of helping people reduce communication apprehension should be restricted to instances in which a true communication skills deficit actually exists. It is not enough that the people who are to receive treatment think they are skill deficient, they must actually be so. If they are adequately skilled, but think they aren't, the problem is one of inappropriate cognitive processing and cognitive restructuring should be the treatment of choice. If they have deficient skills, but think their skills are satisfactory, *no treatment* is called for. Such individuals will lack the commitment to work with the professional helper and, consequently, no positive outcome should be expected.

One final word of caution concerning the use of skills training. Improved skills can only be expected to result in areas in which specific skills training is provided. By this we mean that skills training does not generalize. As an illustration, consider skills training for public speaking. If specific training in how to construct a good introduction to a speech is provided, we should expect the person after training to be able to prepare a better introduction. However, we should not expect the person to be able to prepare a better conclusion or to prepare better for a formal interview. Such skill generalization simply does not occur.

As a result, we can not expect any generalized reduction in communication apprehension to be produced by skills training. To the extent that apprehension stems from deficient skills, with specific skills training we can expect to reduce only apprehension related to that particular skill area. Thus, skills training involving formal interviews may help reduce apprehension about communicating in interviews, but cannot be expected to reduce apprehension about communicating in any other communication context.

Skills training as a method of reducing communication apprehension, then, has limited usefulness. When a person has high communication apprehension about a variety of communication contexts, systematic desensitization or cognitive restructuring are the methods that should be used for treatment. If, however, the individual has high apprehension about only one type of communication context and has deficient skills in that area, skills training may be very helpful.

An effective skills training program normally will include the following components: (1) identification of the specific skill deficiency (or deficiencies); (2) determining subskills making up a larger area of deficient skill; (3) establishing attainable goals for acquiring new skills; (4) observing in a skilled individual model the behavior to be learned; (5) developing a cognitive understanding of the nature of the skill to be learned (becoming able to explain verbally what is to be done); (6) practicing the new behavior in a controlled, nonthreatening environment where the helper can observe the behavior and suggest methods of improvement; and (7) practicing the new behavior in the natural environment. While not all skills training programs include all of these components, most effective ones do. Many programs include other components as well. Sometimes the additional components are similar to cognitive restructuring in that they are directed toward creating a better understanding of the communication process and eliminating negative beliefs that may spawn negative self-statements.

A FINAL WORD

We have stressed throughout this book that communication apprehension, communication avoidance, and communication effectiveness are highly interrelated. Communication apprehension, whether generalized across communication contexts, specific to a given context, specific to a given receiver or group of receivers, or generated by a specific situation, is probably the single most important factor in ineffective communication.

A person who experiences communication apprehension is not the strange exception—almost all of us experience such apprehension at some time or other; some of us more often than others. For those of us who experience it only rarely, it is not a major problem in our lives. For those of us who experience it to the point that it interferes with our daily lives or stands in our way of personal or professional success, we need not accept this state of affairs as something we have to live with.

As we have noted in this chapter, communication apprehension can be substantially reduced by a variety of methods and has been so reduced for literally thousands of individuals already. Many schools and colleges have programs based on the methods discussed in this chapter available at little or no cost. Where no such program is available, except in very low population areas, it is almost certain that a clinical psychologist trained in the use of systematic desensitization and/or cognitive restructuring will be available locally who can provide the help needed. In addition, an increasing number of communication professors and specialists who can provide such help are becoming available. The minimal cost of obtaining such help will be far out weighed by the benefits obtained. If you feel you might benefit from such help, do not hesitate to seek it.

Selected References

Andersen, P. A., Andersen, J. F., and Garrison, J. P. (1978). Singing apprehension and talking apprehension: The development of two constructs. *Sign Language Studies, 19,* 155–186.

Bandura, A. (1977). Self-efficacy: Toward a unifying theory of behavior and behavior change. *Psychological Review, 84,* 191–215.

Bandura, A., Blanchard, E. B., and Ritter, B. (1969). The relative efficacy of desensitization and modeling approaches for inducing behavioral, affective, and attitudinal change. *Journal of Personality and Social Psychology, 13,* 173–199.

Barker, L., Cegala, D. J., Kibler, R. J. and Wahlers, K. J. (1972). Hypnosis and the reduction of speech anxiety. *Central States Speech Journal, 23,* 28–35.

Bashore, D. N., McCroskey, J. C., and Andersen, J. F. (1976). The relationship between communication apprehension and academic achievement among college students. *Human Communication Research, 3,* 73–81.

Beatty, M. J. (1984). Physiological assessment. In J. A. Daly and J. C. McCroskey (Eds.), *Avoiding communication: Shyness, reticence, and communication apprehension,* Beverly Hills, CA: Sage.

Beatty, M. J. and Behnke, R. R. (1980). An assimilation theory perspective of communication apprehension. *Human Communication Research, 6,* 319–325.

Behnke, R. R. and Beatty, M. J. (1981). A cognitive-physiological model of speech anxiety. *Communication Monographs, 48,* 158–163.

Bell, R. A. and Daly, J. A. (1984). The affinity-seeking function of communication. *Communication Monographs, 51,* 91-115.

Bem, S. L. (1974). The measurement of psychological androgyny. *Journal of Consulting and Clinical Psychology, 42,* 155–162.

Berger, B. A., McCroskey, J. C., and Richmond, V. P. (1984). Communication apprehension and shyness. In W. N. Tindall, R. S. Beardsley, and F. R. Curtiss (Eds.), *Communication in pharmacy practice: A practical guide for students and practitioners.* Philadelphia, PA: Lea and Febiger.

Berlo, D. K. (1960). *The process of communication.* New York: Holt, Rinehart and Winston.

Booth-Butterfield, S. (1988). The effect of communication apprehension and anticipated interaction on student recall of information. Dissertation completed at West Virginia University.

Burgoon, J. K. (1976). The unwillingness-to-communicate scale: Development and validation. *Communication Monographs, 43,* 60–69.

Buss, A. H. (1980). *Self-consciousness and social anxiety.* San Francisco: W. H. Freeman.

Buss, A. H. (1984). A conception of shyness. In J. A. Daly and J. C. McCroskey (Eds.), *Avoiding communication: Shyness, reticence, and communication apprehension,* Beverly Hills, CA: Sage.

Cheek, J. M., and Busch, C. M. (1981). The influence of shyness on loneliness in a new situation. *Personality and Social Psychology Bulletin, 7,* 572–577.

Clevenger, T., Jr. (1959). A synthesis of experimental research in stage fright. *Quarterly Journal of Speech, 45,* 134–145.

Daly, J. A., and Hailey, J. L. (1983). Putting the situation into writing research: Situation parameters of writing apprehension as disposition and state. In R. E. Beach and L. Bidwell (Eds.), *New directions in composition research.* New York: Guilford.

Daly, J. A., and McCroskey, J. C. (Eds.) (1984). *Avoiding communication: Shyness, reticence, and communication apprehension.* Beverly Hills, CA: Sage.

Daly, J. A., and Miller, M. D. (1975). The empirical development of an instrument to measure writing apprehension. *Research in the Teaching of English, 9,* 242–249.

Daly, J. A., McCroskey, J. C., and Richmond, V. P. (1977). The relationships between vocal activity and perception of communicators in small group interaction. *Western Speech Communication Journal, 41,* 175–187.

Daly, J. A., Richmond, V. P., and Leth, S. (1979). Social communication anxiety and the personnel selection process: Testing the similarity effect in selection decisions. *Human Communication Research, 6,* 18–32.

Ellis, A. (1962). *Reason and emotion in psychotherapy.* New York: Stuart.

Freimuth, V. S. (1982). Communication apprehension in the classroom. In L. Barker (Ed.), *Communication in the classroom.* Englewood Cliffs, NJ: Prentice-Hall.

Fremouw, W. J. (1984). Cognitive-behavioral therapies for modification of communication apprehension. In J. A. Daly and J. C. McCroskey (Eds.), *Avoiding communication: Shyness, reticence, and communication apprehension.* Beverly Hills, CA: Sage.

Gilkinson, H. (1942). Social fears as reported by students in college speech classes. *Speech Monographs, 9,* 141–160.

Gorham, J. (1988). The relationship between verbal teacher immediacy behaviors and student learning. *Communication Education, 37,* 40–53.

Goss, B., Thompson, M., and Olds, S. (1978). Behavioral support for systematic desensitization for communication apprehension. *Human Communication Research, 4,* 158–163.

Hays, D. P., and Meltzer, L. (1972). Interpersonal judgments based on talkativeness I: Fact or artifact? *Sociometry, 33,* 538–561.

Hoffman, J., and Sprague, J. (1982). A survey of reticence and communication apprehension treatment programs at U.S. colleges and universities. *Communication Education, 31,* 185–193.

Klopf, D. W. (1984). Cross-cultural apprehension research: A summary of pacific basin studies. In J. A. Daly and J. C. McCroskey (Eds.), *Avoiding communication: Shyness, reticence, and communication apprehension.* Beverly Hills, CA: Sage.

Lashbrook, W. B. , Knutson, P. K., Parsley, M. L., and Wenberg, J. R. (1976) November). An empirical examination of versatility as a consequent of perceived social style. Paper presented at the annual convention of the Western States Speech Communication Association, Phoenix, AZ.

McCroskey, J. C. (1970). Measures of communication-bound anxiety. *Speech Monographs, 37,* 269–277.

McCroskey, J. C. (1972). The implementation of a large-scale program of systematic desensitization for communication apprehension. *Speech Teacher, 21,* 255–264.

McCroskey, J. C. (1977). Classroom consequences of communication apprehension. *Communication Education, 26,* 27–33.

McCroskey, J. C. (1977). Oral communication apprehension: A summary of recent theory and research. *Human Communication Research, 4,* 78–96.

McCroskey, J. C. (1977). *Quiet children and the classroom teacher.* Urbana, IL: Educational Resources Information Center.

McCroskey, J. C. (1978). Validity of the PRCA as an index of oral communication apprehension. *Communication Monographs, 45,* 192–203.

McCroskey, J. C. (1980). On communication competence and communication apprehension: A response to Page. *Communication Education, 29,* 109–111.

McCroskey, J. C. (1980). Quiet children in the classroom: On helping not hurting. *Communication Education, 29,* 239–244.

McCroskey, J. C. (1982). Oral communication apprehension: A reconceptualization. In M. Burgoon (Ed.), *Communication Yearbook, 6.* Beverly Hills, CA: Sage.

McCroskey, J. C. (1984). The communication apprehension perspective. In J. A. Daly and J. C. McCroskey (Eds.), *Avoiding communication: Shyness, reticence, and communication apprehension,* Beverly Hills, CA: Sage.

McCroskey, J. C. (1984). Self-report measurement. In J. A. Daly and J. C. McCroskey (Eds.), *Avoiding communication: Shyness, reticence, and communication apprehension,* Beverly Hills, CA: Sage.

McCroskey, J. C. (1986). *An introduction to rhetorical communication,* 5th ed. Englewood Cliffs, NJ: Prentice-Hall.

McCroskey, J. C., and McCroskey L. L. (1986). Self-report as an approach to measuring communication competence. Paper presented at the annual convention of the Central States Speech Communication Association, Cincinnati, OH.

McCroskey, J. C., and Richmond, V. P. (1978). Community size as a predictor of development of communication apprehension: Replication and extension. *Communication Education,* 27, 212–219.

McCroskey, J. C., and Richmond, V. P. (1979). The impact of communication apprehension on individuals in organizations. *Communication Quarterly,* 27, 55–61.

McCroskey, J. C., and Richmond, V. P. (1980). *The quiet ones: Shyness and communication apprehension.* Scottsdale, AZ: Gorsuch Scarisbrick.

McCroskey, J. C., and Richmond, V. P. (1982). *The quiet ones: Communication apprehension and shyness,* 2nd ed. Scottsdale, AZ: Gorsuch Scarisbrick.

McCroskey, J. C., and Richmond, V. P. (1987). Willingness to communicate. In J.C. McCroskey and J. A. Daly (Eds.), *Personality and interpersonal communication.* Beverly Hills, CA: Sage.

McCroskey, J. C., and Richmond, V. P. (1988). Communication apprehension and small group communication. In R. S. Cathcart and L. A. Samovar (Eds.), *Small group communication: A reader.* Dubuque, Iowa: Wm. C. Brown.

McCroskey, J. C., and Wheeless, L. R. (1976). *Introduction to human communication.* Boston: Allyn and Bacon.

McCroskey, J. C., Andersen, J. F., Richmond, V. P., and Wheeless, L. R. (1981). Communication apprehension of elementary and secondary students and teachers. *Communication Education, 30,* 122–132.

McCroskey, J. C., Fayer, J., and Richmond, V. P. (1985). Don't speak to me in English: Communication apprehension among Puerto Rican students. *Communication Quarterly, 33,* 185–192.

McCroskey, J. C., Larson, C. E., and Knapp, M. L. (1971). An introduction to interpersonal communication. Englewood Cliffs, NJ: Prentice-Hall.

McCroskey, J. C., Ralph, D. C., and Barrick, J. E. (1968, December). The effect of systematic desensitization on speech anxiety. Paper presented at the annual convention of the Speech Association of America, Chicago, IL.

McCroskey, J. C., Ralph, D. C., and Barrick, J. E. (1970). The effect of systematic desensitization on speech anxiety. *Speech Teacher, 19,* 32–36.

McCroskey, J. C., Richmond, V. P., and Stewart, R. (1986). One-on-one: The foundations of interpersonal communication. Englewood Cliffs, NJ: Prentice- Hall.

McCroskey, J. C., Richmond, V. P., Berger, B. A., and Baldwin, H. J. (1983). H o w to make a good thing worse: A comparison of approaches to helping students overcome communication apprehension. *Communication, 12,* 213–220.

McCroskey, J. C., Richmond, V. P., Daly, J. A., and Falcione, R. L. (1977). Studies of the relationship between communication apprehension and self-esteem. *Human Communication Research, 3,* 269–277.

Mehrabian, A. (1971). *Silent messages.* Belmont, CA: Wadsworth.

Meichenbaum, D. (1977). *Cognitive behavior modification.* New York: Plenum.

Merrill, D. W., and Reid, R.(1981). *Personal styles and effective performance: Make your style work for you.* Radnor, PA: Chilton Book.

Miller, G. R., and Steinberg, M. (1975). *Between people: A new analysis of interpersonal communication.* Chicago: Science Research Associates.

Mortensen, D. C., Arntson, P. H., and Lustig, M. (1977). The measurement of verbal predispositions: Scale development and application. *Human Communication Research, 3,* 146–158.

Newton, C. K. (1986). *The social style profile: A perspective on its development.* Denver, CO: The TRACOM Corporation/A Reed Publishing USA Company.

Paul, G. L. (1966). *Insight vs. desensitization in psychotherapy: An experiment in anxiety reduction.* Stanford, CA: Stanford University Press.

Payne, S. K., and Richmond, V. P. (1984). A bibliography of related theory and research. In J. A. Daly and J. C. McCroskey (Eds.), *Avoiding communication: Shyness, reticence, and communication apprehension,* Beverly Hills, CA: Sage.

Phillips, G. M. (1968). Reticence: Pathology of the normal speaker. *Speech Monographs, 35,* 39–49.

Phillips, G. M. (1977). Rhetoritherapy versus the medical model: Dealing with reticence. *Communication Education, 26,* 34–43.

Pilkonis, P., Heape, C., and Klein, R. H. (1980). Treating shyness and other relationship difficulties in psychiatric outpatients. *Communication Education, 29,* 250–255.

Richmond, V. P. (1978). The relationship between trait and state communication apprehension and interpersonal perception during acquaintance stages. *Human Communication Research, 4,* 338–349.

Richmond, V. P. (1980). Monomorphic and polymorphic opinion leadership within a relatively closed communication system. *Human Communication Research, 6,* 111–116.

Richmond, V. P. (1984). Implications of quietness: Some facts and speculations. In J. A. Daly and J. C. McCroskey (Eds.), *Avoiding communication: Shyness, reticence, and communication apprehension.* Beverly Hills, CA: Sage.

Richmond, V. P., Beatty, M., and Dyba, P. (1985). Shyness and popularity: Children's views. *Western Speech Communication Journal, 49,* 116–125.

Richmond, V. P., Gorham, J. S., and Furio, B. J. (1987). Affinity-seeking communication in collegiate female-male relationships. *Communication Quarterly, 35,* 334–348.

Richmond, V. P., Gorham, J. S., and McCroskey, J. C. (1987). The relationship between selected immediacy behaviors and cognitive learning. In M. McLaughlin (Ed.), *Communication Yearbook 10.* Beverly Hills, CA: Sage.

Richmond, V. P., McCroskey, J. C., and Davis, L. M. (1986). Communication apprehension and affinity-seeking in superior-subordinate relationships. *World Communication, 15,* 41–54.

Richmond, V. P., McCroskey, J. C., and Davis, L. M. (1986). The relationship of supervisor use of power and affinity seeking strategies with subordinate satisfaction. *Communication Quarterly, 34,* 178–193.

Richmond, V. P., McCroskey, J. C., and Payne, S. K. (1987). *Nonverbal behavior in interpersonal relationships.* Englewood Cliffs, NJ: Prentice-Hall.

Shannon, C. E., and Weaver, W. (1949). *The mathematical theory of communication.* Urbana, IL: University of Illinois Press.

Spielberger, C. D. (Ed.) (1966). *Anxiety and behavior.* New York: Academic Press.

Spielberger, C. D. (1966). Theory and research on anxiety. In C. D. Spielberger (Ed.), *Anxiety and behavior.* New York: Academic Press.

Wheeless, V. E., and Dierks-Stewart, K. (1981). The psychometric properties of the Bem sex-role inventory: Questions concerning reliability and validity. *Communication Quarterly, 29,* 173–186.

Wolpe, J. (1958). *Psychotherapy by reciprocal inhibition.* Stanford, CA: Stanford University Press.

Zimbardo, P. G. (1977). *Shyness: What it is, what to do about it.* Reading, MA: Addison-Wesley.

Zimbardo, P. G. (1981). *The shy child.* New York: McGraw Hill.

Index

Shyness Scale (SS)

DIRECTIONS: The following fourteen statements refer to talking with other people. If the statement describes you very well, circle "YES." If it somewhat describes you, circle "yes." If you are not sure whether it describes you or not, or if you do not understand the statement, circle "?." If the statement is a poor description of you, circle "no." If the statement is a very poor description of you, circle "NO." There are no right or wrong answers. Work quickly; record your first impression.

1. I am a shy person.	YES yes ? no NO
2. Other people think I talk a lot.	YES yes ? no NO
3. I am a very talkative person.	YES yes ? no NO
4. Other people think I am shy.	YES yes ? no NO
5. I talk a lot.	YES yes ? no NO
6. I tend to be very quiet in class.	YES yes ? no NO
7. I don't talk much.	YES yes ? no NO
8. I talk more than most people.	YES yes ? no NO
9. I am a quiet person.	YES yes ? no NO
10. I talk more in a small group (3–6) than others do.	YES yes ? no NO
11. Most people talk more than I do.	YES yes ? no NO
12. Other people think I am very quiet.	YES yes ? no NO
13. I talk more in class than most people do.	YES yes ? no NO
14. Most people are more shy than I am.	YES yes ? no NO

SCORING: YES = 1, yes = 2, ? = 3, no = 4, NO = 5.

Please score your responses as follows:

1. Add the scores for items 1, 4, 6, 7, 9, 11, and 12.
2. Add the scores for items 2, 3, 5, 8, 10, 13, and 14.
3. Complete the following formula: Shyness = 42 - (total from step 1) + (total from step 2).

Scores above 52 indicate a high level of shyness. Scores below 32 indicate a low level of shyness. Scores between 32 and 52 indicate a moderate level of shyness.

Willingness to Communicate Scale (WTC)

DIRECTIONS: Below are twenty situations in which a person might choose to communicate or not to communicate. Presume you have *completely free choice*. Indicate the percentage of time you would choose *to communicate* in each type of situation. Indicate in the space at the left what percent of the time you would choose to communicate.
0 = never, 100 = always

_____	1. *Talk with a service station attendent.
_____	2. *Talk with a physician.
_____	3. Present a talk to a group of strangers.
_____	4. Talk with an acquaintance while standing in line.
_____	5. *Talk with a salesperson in a store.
_____	6. Talk in a large meeting of friends.
_____	7. *Talk with a policeman/policewoman.
_____	8. Talk in a small group of strangers.
_____	9. Talk with a friend while standing in line.
_____	10. *Talk with a waiter/waitress in a restaurant.
_____	11. Talk in a large meeting of acquaintances.
_____	12. Talk with a stranger while standing in line.
_____	13. *Talk with a secretary.
_____	14. Present a talk to a group of friends.
_____	15. Talk in a small group of acquaintances.
_____	16. *Talk with a garbage collector.
_____	17. Talk in a large meeting of strangers.
_____	18. *Talk with a spouse (or girl/boy friend).
_____	19. Talk in a small group of friends.
_____	20. Present a talk to a group of acquaintances.

*Filler item

The WTC is designed to indicate how willing you are to communicate in a variety of contexts with different types of receivers. The higher your score for the WTC total score, the more willing you are to communicate generally. Similarly, the higher your given subscore for a type of context or audience, the more willing you are to communicate in that type of context or with that type of audience.

The WTC permits computation of one total score and seven subscores. The sucbscores relate to willingness to communicate in each of four common communication contexts and with three types of audiences. To compute your scores, merely add your scores for each item and divide by the number indicated below.

Subscore Desired	Scoring Formula
Group discussion	Add scores for items 8, 15, and 19; then divide by 3.
Meetings	Add scores for items 6, 11, and 17; then divide by 3.
Interpersonal conversations	Add scores for items 4, 9, and 12; then divide by 3.
Public speaking	Add scores for items 3, 14, and 20; then divide by 3.
Stranger	Add scores for items 3, 8, 12, and 17; then divide by 4.
Acquaintance	Add scores for items 4, 11,15, and 20; then divide by 4.
Friend	Add scores for items 6, 9, 14, and 19; then divide by 4.

To compute the total WTC scores, add the subscores for stranger, acquaintance, and friend. Then divide by 3.

Norms for WTC Scores

Group discussion	>89 High WTC <57 Low WTC
Meetings	>80 High WTC <39 Low WTC

Interpersonal conversations   >94 High WTC
                               <64 Low WTC

Public speaking   >78 High WTC
                               <33 Low WTC

Stranger   >63 High WTC
                               <18 Low WTC

Acquaintance   >92 High WTC
                               <57 Low WTC

Friend   >99 High WTC
                               <71 Low WTC

Total WTC   >82 High Overall WTC
                               <52 Low Overall WTC

Writing Apprehension Test (WAT)

DIRECTIONS: Below are a series of statements about writing. There are no right or wrong answers to these statements. Please indicate the degree to which each statement applies to you by marking whether you (1) strongly agree, (2) agree, (3) are uncertain, (4) disagree, or (5) strongly disagree with the statement. While some of these statements may seem repetitious, take your time and try to be as honest as possible.

1. I avoid writing.
2. I have no fear of my writing being evaluated.
3. I look forward to writing down my ideas.
4. My mind seems to go blank when I start to work on a composition.
5. Expressing ideas through writing seems to be a waste of time.
6. I would enjoy submitting my writing to magazines for evaluation and publication.
7. I like to write my ideas down.
8. I feel confident in my ability to clearly express my ideas in writing.
9. I like to have my friends read what I have written.
10. I'm nervous about writing.
11. People seem to enjoy what I write.
12. I enjoy writing.
13. I never seem to be able to clearly write down my ideas.
14. Writing is a lot of fun.
15. I like seeing my thoughts on paper.
16. Discussing my writing with others is an enjoyable experience.

_____ 17. It's easy for me to write good compositions.
_____ 18. I don't think I write as well as most other people.
_____ 19. I don't like my compositions to be evaluated.
_____ 20. I'm no good at writing.

To determine your score on the WAT, complete the following steps:

1. Add the scores for items 1, 4, 5, 10, 13, 18, 19, and 20.
2. Add the scores for items 2, 3, 6, 7, 8, 9, 11, 12, 14, 15, 16, and 17.
3. Complete the following formula: WAT = 48 − (total from step 1) + (total from step 2).

Your score should be between 20 and 100. If your score is below 20 or above 100, you have made a mistake in computing the score. See Chapter 4, "The Nature of CA," for interpretation of WAT score.

Test of Singing Apprehension (TOSA)

DIRECTIONS: This instrument is composed of twenty statements concerning feelings about singing and about communicating with other people. Please indicate the degree to which each statement applies to you by marking a number in the left hand column. Mark the degree to which each statement applies as follows: (1) strongly agree, (2) agree, (3) undecided, (4) disagree, (5) strongly disagree. There are no right or wrong answers. Work quickly; just record your first impression. We realize that many items may seem similar, but this is necessary since words have different meanings to different people. Please treat each question independently and respond to each item honestly.

_____ 1. I look forward to singing along with my friends.
_____ 2. The pitch of my voice makes me embarrassed to sing.
_____ 3. Singing in front of others causes me to be embarrassed.
_____ 4. I'm afraid to sing aloud with friends.
_____ 5. I am tense and nervous while singing at group gatherings.
_____ 6. When singing, my posture feels strained and nervous.
_____ 7. I look forward to an opportunity to sing in public.
_____ 8. I have no fear of singing in a group.
_____ 9. I feel I sing on key more than most people do.
_____ 10. I like to get involved in group singing.
_____ 11. I always avoid singing in public if possible.
_____ 12. I look forward to singing in front of my friends.
_____ 13. When I sing in front of others, my throat tightens up.
_____ 14. I dislike using my voice musically.
_____ 15. I feel relaxed and comfortable while singing.
_____ 16. I am afraid to sing in a group.

_____ 17. I am fearful and tense all the while I am singing a song before a group of people.

_____ 18. I sing less because I'm musically shy.

_____ 19. I have trouble staying on key while singing in a group.

_____ 20. I am able to overcome any initial nervousness as soon as I start singing.

To determine your TOSA score, complete the following steps:

1. Add the scores for items 2, 3, 4, 5, 6, 11, 13, 14, 16, 17, 18, and 19.
2. Add the scores for items 1, 7, 8, 9, 10, 12, 15, and 20.
3. Complete the following formula: TOSA = 72 − (total from step 1) + (total from step 2).

Your score should be between 20 and 100. If your score is below 20 or above 100, you have made a mistake in computing the score.

Scores above 68 indicate a high level of singing apprehension. Scores below 37 indicate a low level of singing apprehension. The range of scores between 68 and 37 represent the "normal range" of apprehension about singing.

Personal Report of Communication Apprehension (PRCA-24)

DIRECTIONS: This instrument is composed of twenty-four statements concerning feelings about communicating with other people. Please indicate the degree to which each statement applies to you by marking whether you (1) strongly agree, (2) agree, (3) are undecided, (4) disagree, or (5) strongly disagree. Please just record your first impression.

_____ 1. I dislike participating in group discussions.

_____ 2. Generally, I am comfortable while participating in group discussions.

_____ 3. I am tense and nervous while participating in group discussions.

_____ 4. I like to get involved in group discussions.

_____ 5. Engaging in a group discussion with new people makes me tense and nervous.

_____ 6. I am calm and relaxed while participating in group discussions.

_____ 7. Generally, I am nervous when I have to participate in a meeting.

_____ 8. Usually I am calm and relaxed while participating in meetings.

_____ 9. I am very calm and relaxed when I am called upon to express an opinion at a meeting.

_____ 10. I am afraid to express myself at meetings.

_____ 11. Communicating at meetings usually makes me uncomfortable.

_____ 12. I am very relaxed when answering questions at a meeting.

_____ 13. While participating in a conversation with a new acquaintance, I feel very nervous.
_____ 14. I have no fear of speaking up in conversations.
_____ 15. Ordinarily I am very tense and nervous in conversations.
_____ 16. Ordinarily I am very calm and relaxed in conversations.
_____ 17. While conversing with a new acquaintance, I feel very relaxed.
_____ 18. I'm afraid to speak up in conversations.
_____ 19. I have no fear of giving a speech.
_____ 20. Certain parts of my body feel very tense and rigid while giving a speech.
_____ 21. I feel relaxed while giving a speech.
_____ 22. My thoughts become confused and jumbled when I am giving a speech.
_____ 23. I face the prospect of giving a speech with confidence.
_____ 24. While giving a speech, I get so nervous I forget facts I really know.

The PRCA permits computation of one total score and four subscores. The subscores are related to communication apprehension in each of four common communication contexts: group discussions, meetings, interpersonal conversations, and public speaking. To compute your scores merely add or subtract your scores for each item as indicated below.

Subscore Desired	Scoring Formula
Group discussion	18 + scores for items 2,4, and 6; − scores for items 1, 3, and 5.
Meetings	18 + scores for items 8, 9, and 12; − scores for items 7, 10, and 11.
Interpersonal conversations	18 + scores for items 14, 16, and 17; − scores for items 13, 15, and 18.
Public speaking	18 + scores for items 19, 21, and 23; − scores for items 20, 22, and 24.

To obtain your total score for the PRCA, simply add your four subscores together. Your score should range between 24 and 120. If your score is below 24 or above 120, you have made a mistake in computing the score. See Chapter 4, "Traitlike CA," for interpretation of overall PRCA score.

Scores on the four contexts (Groups, Meetings, Interpersonal conversations, and Public speaking) can range from a low of 6 to a high of 30. Any score above 18 indicates some degree of apprehension. If your score is above 18 for the Public speaking context, you are like the overwhelming majority of Americans.

APPENDIX F

Personal Report of Public Speaking Anxiety (PRPSA)

DIRECTIONS: This instrument is composed of thirty-four statements concerning feelings about communicating with other people. Indicate the degree to which the statements apply to you by marking whether you (1) strongly agree, (2) agree, (3) are undecided, (4) disagree, or (5) strongly disagree with each statement. Work quickly; just record your first impression.

_____ 1. While preparing for giving a speech, I feel tense and nervous.

_____ 2. I feel tense when I see the words *speech* and *public speech* on a course outline when studying.

_____ 3. My thoughts become confused and jumbled when I am giving a speech.

_____ 4. Right after giving a speech I feel that I have had a pleasant experience.

_____ 5. I get anxious when I think about a speech coming up.

_____ 6. I have no fear of giving a speech.

_____ 7. Although I am nervous just before starting a speech, I soon settle down after starting and feel calm and comfortable.

_____ 8. I look forward to giving a speech.

_____ 9. When the instructor announces a speaking assignment in class, I can feel myself getting tense.

_____ 10. My hands tremble when I am giving a speech.

_____ 11. I feel relaxed while giving a speech.

_____ 12. I enjoy preparing for a speech.

_____ 13. I am in constant fear of forgetting what I prepared to say.

_____ 14. I get anxious if someone asks me something about my topic that I do not know.

_____ 15. I face the prospect of giving a speech with confidence.

_____ 16. I feel that I am in complete possession of myself while giving a speech.

_____ 17. My mind is clear when giving a speech.

_____ 18. I do not dread giving a speech.

_____ 19. I perspire just before starting a speech.

_____ 20. My heart beats very fast just as I start a speech.

_____ 21. I experience considerable anxiety while sitting in the room just before my speech starts.

_____ 22. Certain parts of my body feel very tense and rigid while giving a speech.

_____ 23. Realizing that only a little time remains in a speech makes me very tense and anxious.

_____ 24. While giving a speech I know I can control my feelings of tension and stress.

_____ 25. I breathe faster just before starting a speech.

_____ 26. I feel comfortable and relaxed in the hour or so just before giving a speech.

_____ 27. I do poorer on speeches because I am anxious.

_____ 28. I feel anxious when the teacher announces the date of a speaking assignment.

_____ 29. When I make a mistake while giving a speech, I find it hard to concentrate on the parts that follow.

_____ 30. During an important speech I experience a feeling of help-lessness building up inside me.

_____ 31. I have trouble falling asleep the night before a speech.

_____ 32. My heart beats very fast while I present a speech.

_____ 33. I feel anxious while waiting to give my speech.

_____ 34. While giving a speech I get so nervous I forget facts I really know.

To determine your score on the PRPSA, complete the following steps:

1. Add the scores for items 1, 2, 3, 5, 9, 10, 13, 14, 19, 20, 21, 22, 23, 25, 27, 28, 29, 30, 31, 32, 33, and 34.
2. Add the scores for items 4, 6, 7, 8, 11, 12, 15, 16, 17, 18, 24, and 26.
3. Complete the following formula: PRPSA = 132 − (total = from step 1) + (total from step 2).

Your score should range between 34 and 170. If your score is below 34 or above 170, you have made a mistake in computing the score. See Chapter 4, "Context-Based CA," for interpretation of PRPSA score.

Communication Apprehension in Generalized Contexts

DIRECTIONS: This instrument is composed of fifty statements concerning your feelings about commuicating with other people, divided into five categories. Please indicate in the space provided the degree to which each statement applies to you by marking whether you (1) strongly agree, (2) agree, (3) are undecided, (4) disagree, or (5) strongly disagree with each statement. There are no right or wrong answers. Many statements are similar to other statements. Do not be concerned because of this. Work quickly; just record your first impression.

General

_____ 1. When communicating, I generally am calm and relaxed.

_____ 2. Generally, communication causes me to be anxious and apprehensive.

_____ 3. I find the prospect of speaking mildly pleasant.

_____ 4. When communicating, my posture feels strained and unnatural.

_____ 5. In general, communication makes me uncomfortable.

_____ 6. For the most part, I like to communicate with other people.

_____ 7. I dislike using my body and voice expressively.

_____ 8. I feel that I am more fluent when talking to people than most other people are.

_____ 9. When communicating, I generally am tense and nervous.

_____ 10. I feel relaxed and comfortable while speaking.

Group Discussions

_____ 11. I am afraid to express myself in a group.

_____ 12. I dislike participating in group discussions.

_____ 13. Generally, I am comfortable while participating in a group discussions.

_____ 14. I am tense and nervous while participating in group discussions.

_____ 15. I have no fear about expressing myself in a group.

_____ 16. Engaging in a group discussion with new people is very pleasant.

_____ 17. Generally, I am uncomfortable while participating in a group discussion.

_____ 18. I like to get involved in group discussions.

_____ 19. Engaging in a group discussion with new people makes me tense and nervous.

_____ 20. I am calm and relaxed while participating in group discussions.

Meetings

_____ 21. I look forward to expressing my opinions at meetings.

_____ 22. I am self-conscious when I am called upon to express an opinion at a meeting.

_____ 23. Generally, I am nervous when I have to participate in a meeting.

_____ 24. Communicating in meetings generally makes me feel good.

_____ 25. Usually I am calm and relaxed while participating in meetings.

_____ 26. I am self-conscious when I am called upon to answer a question at a meeting.

_____ 27. I am very calm and relaxed when I am called upon to express an opinion at a meeting.

_____ 28. I am afraid to express myself at meetings.

_____ 29. Communicating in meetings generally makes me feel uncomfortable.

_____ 30. I am very relaxed when answering questions at a meeting.

Interpersonal Conversations

_____ 31. While participating in a conversation with a new acquaintance I feel very nervous.

_____ 32. I have no fear of speaking up in conversations.

_____ 33. Talking with one other person very often makes me nervous.

_____ 34. Ordinarily, I am very tense and nervous in conversations.

_____ 35. Conversing with people who hold positions of authority causes me to be fearful and tense.

_____ 36. Generally, I am very relaxed while talking with one other person.

_____ 37. Ordinarily, I am very calm and relaxed in conversations.

_____ 38. While conversing with a new acquaintance I feel very relaxed.

_____ 39. I am relaxed while conversing with people who hold positions of authority.

_____ 40. I am afraid to speak up in conversations.

Public Speeches

_____ 41. I have no fear of giving a speech.

_____ 42. I look forward to giving a speech.

_____ 43. Certain parts of my body feel very tense and rigid while giving a speech.

_____ 44. I feel relaxed while giving a speech.

_____ 45. Giving a speech makes me anxious.

_____ 46. My thoughts become confused and jumbled when I am giving a speech.

_____ 47. I face the prospect of giving a speech with confidence.

_____ 48. While giving a speech I get so nervous I forget facts I really know.

_____ 49. Giving a speech really scares me.

_____ 50. While giving a speech I know I can control my feelings of tension and stress.

SCORING:

General = 30 – (total of items 2, 4, 5, 7, 9) + (total of items 1, 3, 6, 8, 10)

Group = 30 – (total of items 11, 12, 14, 17, 19) + (total of items 13, 15, 16, 18, 20)

Meetings = 30 – (total of items 22, 23, 26, 28, 29) + (total of items 21, 24, 25, 27, 30)

Interpersonal = 30 – (total of items 31, 33, 34, 35, 40) + (total of items 32, 36, 37, 38, 39)

Public = 30 – (total of items 43, 45, 46, 48, 49) + (total of items 41, 42, 44, 47, 50)

See Chapter 4, "Context-Based CA," for interpretation of results.

APPENDIX H

Situational Communication Apprehension Measure (SCAM)

DIRECTIONS: Please complete the following questionnaire about how you felt the last time you interacted with someone who had a supervisory role over you. Mark 7 (in the space before the statement) if the statement is extremely accurate for how you felt, 6 if moderately accurate, 5 if somewhat accurate, 4 if neither accurate nor inaccurate, 3 if somewhat inaccurate, 2 if moderately inaccurate, or 1 if extremely inaccurate. There are no right or wrong answers. Just respond to the items quickly to describe as accurately as you can how you felt while interacting with a person who had a supervisory role over you (for example, a teacher).

_____	1. I was apprehensive.	_____	11. I was bothered.
_____	2. I was disturbed.	_____	12. I felt satisfied.
_____	3. I felt peaceful.	_____	13. I felt safe.
_____	4. I was loose.	_____	14. I was flustered.
_____	5. I felt uneasy.	_____	15. I was cheerful.
_____	6. I was self-assured.	_____	16. I felt happy.
_____	7. I was fearful.	_____	17. I felt dejected.
_____	8. I was ruffled.	_____	18. I was pleased.
_____	9. I felt jumpy.	_____	19. I felt good.
_____	10. I was composed.	_____	20. I was unhappy.

To determine your score on the SCAM, complete the following steps:

1. Add the scores for items 3, 4, 6, 10, 12, 13, 15, 16, 18, and 19.
2. Add the scores for items 1, 2, 5, 7, 8, 9, 11, 14, 17, and 20.

3. Complete the following formula: SCAM = 80 – (total from step 1) + (total from step 2).

Your score should be between 20 and 140. If your score is below 20 or above 140, you have made a mistake in computing the score. For interpretation of SCAM see "Audience-Based CA" in Chapter 4.

Self-Perceived Communication Competence Scale (SPCC)

DIRECTIONS: Below are twelve situations in which you might need to communicate. People's abilities to communicate effectively vary a lot, and sometimes the same person is more competent to communicate in one situation than in another. Please indicate how competent you believe you are to communicate in each of the situations described below. Indicate in the space provided at the left of each item your estimate of your competence. Presume 0 = completely incompetent and 100 = completely competent.

_____ 1. Present a talk to a group of strangers.
_____ 2. Talk with an acquaintance.
_____ 3. Talk in a large meeting of friends.
_____ 4. Talk in a small group of strangers.
_____ 5. Talk with a friend.
_____ 6. Talk in a large meeting of acquaintances.
_____ 7. Talk with a stranger.
_____ 8. Present a talk to a group of friends
_____ 9. Talk in a small group of acquaintances.
_____ 10. Talk in a large meeting of strangers.
_____ 11. Talk in a small group of friends.
_____ 12. Present a talk to a group of acquaintances.

SCORING: To compute the subscores, add the percentages for the items indicated and divide the total by the number indicated below.

Public   1 + 8 + 12; divide by 3.

Meeting	3 + 6 + 10; divide by 3.
Group	4 + 9 + 11; divide by 3.
Dyad	2 + 5 + 7; divide by 3.
Stranger	1 + 4 + 7 + 10; divide by 4.
Acquaintance	2 + 6 + 9 + 12; divide by 4.
Friend	3 + 5 + 8 + 11; divide by 4.

To compute the total SPCC score, add the subscores for Stranger, Acquaintance, and Friend. Then divide that total by 3.

	Reliability	Mean	SD	Correlation
Public	.72	68.8	17.8	.50
Meeting	.68	68.8	17.1	.60
Group	.67	76.1	14.6	.52
Dyad	.44	81.1	12.4	.39
Stranger	.87	55.5	23.6	.56
Acquaintance	.84	77.4	15.3	.56
Friend	.78	88.2	11.3	.47
Total	.92	73.7	13.8	.59

Public	>86 High SPCC
	<51 Low SPCC
Meeting	>85 High SPCC
	<51 Low SPCC
Group	>90 High SPCC
	<61 Low SPCC
Dyad	>93 High SPCC
	<68 Low SPCC
Stranger	>79 High SPCC
	<31 Low SPCC
Acquaintance	>92 High SPCC
	<62 Low SPCC
Friend	>99 High SPCC
	<76 Low SPCC
Total SPCC	>87 High SPCC
	<59 Low SPCC

Higher SPCC scores indicate higher self-perceived communication competence with basic communication contexts (public, meeting, group, dyad) and receivers (strangers, acquaintance, friend).

Assertiveness-Responsiveness Measure

The questionnaire below lists twenty personality characteristics. Please indicate the degree to which you believe each of these characteristics *applies to you while interacting with others* by marking whether you (5) strongly agree that it applies, (4) agree that it applies, (3) are undecided, (2) disagree that it applies, or (1) strongly disagree that it applies. There are no right or wrong answers. Work quickly; just record your first impression.

_____	1. helpful
_____	2. defends own beliefs
_____	3. independent
_____	4. responsive to others
_____	5. forceful
_____	6. has strong personality
_____	7. sympathetic
_____	8. compassionate
_____	9. assertive
_____	10. sensitive to the needs of others
_____	11. dominant
_____	12. sincere
_____	13. gentle
_____	14. willing to take a stand
_____	15. warm
_____	16. tender
_____	17. friendly
_____	18. acts as a leader
_____	19. aggressive
_____	20. competitive

To score your responses, add what you marked for each item as follows:

Assertiveness = 2 + 3 + 5 + 6 + 9 + 11 + 14 + 18 + 19 + 20
Responsiveness = 1 + 4 + 7 + 8 + 10 + 12 + 13 + 15 + 16 + 17

Scores above 34 indicate high assertiveness or responsiveness. Scores below 26 indicate low assertiveness or responsiveness. Scores between 26 and 34 indicate moderate levels of assertiveness or responsiveness.

DATE DUE

SEP 1 4 1995		
OCT 1		
OCT 1 0 1996		
DEC 0 5 2001		
DEC 1 9 2001		
FEB 1 9 2002		
MAR 1 2 2002		
MAR 1 4 2006		

HIGHSMITH 45-220